Sound of Heaven, Symphony of Earth

Revised Edition

Ray Hughes

Sound of Heaven, Symphony of Earth
Copyright © 2000 by Ray Hughes
www.selahministries.com

ISBN: 978-06-155171-0-0

Unless otherwise stated, all Scripture quotations are taken from the New King James Version. Copyright © 1979,1980, 1982, Thomas Nelson, Inc.

Edited by Marcus Yoars, Angie Carpenter, Debbie Johnson, Denise Hughes and Nancy Patterson.
Cover art designed by Joe Middleton | designbygenesis.com

Printed in the United States of America

Contents

Introduction

Information or In Formation

This is not a book on the how-to's of praise and worship, nor is it a book about the seven Hebrew words for praise or how to be released into dance. It is not a book about improving musical techniques, developing your song-writing skills, or preparing a Sunday morning worship service. Although much material has been written on those subjects and we have been blessed to grow in all those areas, that is not what this book is about. Rather than an endeavor to simply release more information, *Sound of Heaven, Symphony of Earth* is an endeavor to help bring the body of Christ *in formation.*

We live in the "Information Age," a day of increasing revelation, prophetic insight and sensitivity to the spirit realm. There is certainly no shortage of intellectual stimulation, and spirituality has become almost a flippant byword in some circles. This is a time when science fiction can become science fact overnight. Although this isn't a science book, and I am not a scientist, I do enjoy and take advantage of scientific information. The information I share with you will be based on scientific fact, confessed speculation, and spiritual revelation.

The more I researched and mined the truths for this book, the more I realized there is much we don't yet know about sound and its relationship to the unveiling of God's glory. By no means will I attempt to convince you that I am a scientist or an educator. However, I believe that the Holy Spirit has given me some of the pieces of the puzzle to heaven's sound. I pray that this book will introduce new paths of revelation to those who have an ear to hear and a heart to pursue God.

Worshiping God's Way

I enjoy opportunities to sit around a table and chat with well-informed thinkers, musicians, and students of the Word. What impresses me most are the many different ways God chooses to arrest our lives and overwhelm us with His greatness. Seeing the many ways in which He reveals Himself and His wonder leaves me in a state of wonder. When I see how God shed His light of revelation from generation to generation, I'm continually amazed that God speaks to us in whatever way it takes to keep us hungering and thirsting for a greater knowledge and understanding of Him. It takes true abandonment and bravery to pursue the glory of God when Scripture reveals that no man has seen God and lived. This tells me that no matter who we are, seeking to know and hear God requires a dying process to produce true life. In short, as we die to our ways, we are resurrected to His.

Regretfully, we often insist that we have been given the liberty to worship God in our own way. Truthfully, there is no liberty in that attitude. True liberty comes with the abandonment of self in our worshiping God, freeing us to worship in *His* way, not ours. Dissecting the act of worship and endeavoring to scripturally justify our personal preferences and preach them as convictions never frees anyone. When we are left to worship God in our own way, we simply will not worship God, for our flesh will not allow us to do so. Historically, we see that man's preferences, preached as convictions of the Holy Spirit, bring only greater bondage and limit our liberties in worship.

My desire in this writing is to help eliminate the limitations and bondage to self while encouraging freedom and liberty in worship. May God give us the discernment needed to keep us from making the mistake of embracing limitless boundaries in the name of radical worship, only to find ourselves embracing lawlessness in worship! When lawlessness is embraced, there is no true worship at all. For lawlessness and true worship cannot dwell together in a purified heart. If I ask God for a pure heart while writing this book, and you ask Him for a pure heart while reading it, great things could happen. If some of the writing in this book stretches us beyond where we are and points us to a greater realization of who He is, it will have accomplished its purpose. Be aware that every barricade in scientific research seems to only introduce new possibilities in other areas. At times, it may appear I am attaching a greater importance to the nature of sound than might be necessary. The uniqueness of the subject of sound as seen in Scripture may stir some to be overly conscious, and even extreme, in their evaluation of sound. Let's take caution not to diminish what God is doing through sound.

I encourage all of us to be courageous enough to not only read between the lines, but also to prayerfully give our best ear to hearing what the Spirit of the Lord is saying to us as individuals and as a corporate body. Let's determine to be as courageous and radical as David and Gideon and Joshua and countless others in scripture and history. Their kind of courage is necessary for the time in which we're living. Let's determine in our hearts right now that we will not only read, but *hear*. While great feats have been accomplished through bravery and inspiration, even greater feats can be accomplished through boldness and impartation accompanied with obedience. Let's boldly go before the throne for an impartation of grace.

Chapter One

Snakes in the Hen House

As a child, I had an experience that taught me the difference between bravery and boldness. One day my grandpa commissioned me to go out to the chicken house and bring in the eggs. At that time in my life, this was quite a commissioning, because I had a childish fear of going into the dark, old, chicken house, running my hand under a living creature, and taking what was surely her prized possession. To think of walking in that old tin shack and taking those eggs out from under an animal with a sharp beak, was more than my five-year-old mind could handle. However, at my grandpa's word, I struck out for the chicken house.

I approached the chicken house, and just before I took the last step into the darkness of the little shack, I saw a big black chicken snake crawling across the ground inside the building. If you had been raised in a holler in Kentucky, you were conditioned from birth to know that snakes are not your friends. So I stopped in my tracks, grabbed a tobacco stick by the door and began to pound the side of that old tin chicken house, making a noise that could be heard a mile away. The tin walls were rattling and vibrating with such intensity that the snake immediately realized he was unwelcome. He raced under the walls of the chicken house, and slithered away. When I realized how effective I was at scaring him with the obnoxious pounding, I grabbed the lid off of a feed bucket (which was nothing more than a garbage can full of chicken feed) and began to chase him, banging on the tin lid with the stick. I chased him up the hill, past the apple tree, past the outhouse, past the pond and lost him somewhere in the weeds near the tobacco patch.

Feeling very proud of my brave feat, I went back to the house and told Grandpa what I had done. He smiled and commended me for my bravery with a pat on the back. Then he introduced me to some wisdom and revelation I'll never forget. He said, "You done good, boy. That was a brave thing you did. But he'll be back. You can't keep a snake out of the hen house with noise. The only way to keep a snake out of the hen house is to kill him."

We can apply this story to the church today. In a day of great revelation in the areas of praise, worship, and music, many of these radical releases of praise are biblical and have a tremendous effect in spiritual warfare. However, if all we're doing is making enough noise to get the snake out of the hen house, then we can rest assured he'll be back. Today there's a sound of rattling and thunder in the house of God that's not only running the snakes out, but the chickens as well. As demonstrative and sometimes bizarre expressions of worship have increased so has a sense of lawlessness. Some might celebrate that the house of God is no longer comfortable for chickens.

And okay, let's rejoice that the noise may have saved the chickens life but let's not forget that the snake was spared as well. We're not called to be chickens; we're called to be eagles. Snakes devour chickens. Eagles devour snakes.

The Eye of the Eagle

Another word for volume is amplitude. Spiritual amplitude determines our spiritual attitude. Attitude determines our spiritual altitude. Let's exchange natural amplitude for spiritual amplitude, fleshly attitudes for the attitudes of the Spirit, and the heights of this world for higher altitudes in God. The aggressive sound coming to the church will bring a higher altitude in the spirit realm. Eagles can spot prey from extremely high altitudes. At this new altitude, the church will have the revelatory eye of an eagle needed to become devourers of the slithering snakes in the hen house.

While an eagle flies thousands of feet in the air, a snake or rabbit can move on the ground and draw the attention of the eagle, causing it to swoop down and devour its prey. May God give us the eye of the eagle. With the eye of the eagle comes laser accuracy in the area of discernment, but it's impossible to have effective spiritual discernment without God's wisdom and understanding. If we only have discernment, what good does it do? We must have God's wisdom and understanding to be effective in destroying our true enemies. Much of what we discern to be our enemy is not our enemy at all.

How many times have we discerned things by the so-called "Spirit" and it was only suspicion? This kind of "discernment" that comes without wisdom and understanding can be greatly harmful to others. God wants to fine-tune our spiritual eyes so that we can see His true purposes in praise, worship, and warfare. He will jolt us into reality by taking a stick to the side of the hen house of the church. But He will also do the complete work. He will take the head off the snake! Taking a stick to the side of the hen house is a brave action. Taking the head off of a snake is a bold action. Bravery can be inspired, but boldness requires an impartation of the Holy Spirit.

Through boldness and impartation, the Lord will bring victories and cause us to be effective against our enemies. These victories will assure us of our spiritual authority in Christ, so we don't waste our days in a defensive mode. As we fly as eagles, our concentration ceases to be downward and turns upward. We soar into new heights in God as the Lord bears us up on eagle's wings and brings us to Himself. Wouldn't you love to have a season of soaring higher and higher in God? To break out of the roller-coaster mentality? To get into the third-heaven revelation of whom you were created to be? From that place of revelation, high above the noise of traffic and sound pollution, God invites us to see and hear things that will change this earthly realm. If you desire more revelation than what you're walking in now, let's go together and explore *the sound of heaven, the symphony of earth.*

Chapter Two

The Big Band Sound of the Church

There is a balance between being Spirit-filled and Spirit-skilled. Some of what we credit in worship to the working of the Holy Spirit is simply a justification for a lack of skill. Some years ago a pastor invited me to come and minister at his church. When he picked me up at the airport, I remembered him from a conference I had spoken at earlier in the year. As we drove from the airport, we briefly discussed the wonderful move of God we experienced at that conference, and he voiced a genuine desire to see a release of God in his church. He felt that my being there was timely and that God was doing great things with his musicians. Then he made a request. "In tonight's service our praise team will be ministering, and I would like for you to make mental notes of areas in our music and worship that need attention. The service tomorrow evening will be just for our musicians. I would like for you to share the things you think need improvement and minister in whatever way you consider appropriate."

That night we arrived at the church about ten minutes before the service was to begin. The parking lot was full, and people were filing into the church.

The sounds of musicians tuning up, and the pre-service fellowship rolled down the hall into the pastor's office where we were chatting. He quickly glanced at his watch, grabbed my hand, and prayed a thirty-second prayer for eternal anointing. We were out the door, down the hall and into the auditorium through a side door before I could pop a breath mint. It was there that I was suddenly blasted into the awareness that "The Band" had started. Let me introduce you to "The Band."

On the piano Beverly Baptist was rocking and swatting the keys open-handedly as if she was trying to kill a mouse scurrying on the keyboard. Myrna Methodist sat perched on the organ with her head bowed, one eye closed, a bare left foot waving and consistently bouncing a half-beat behind. Her left hand sustained at least an octave of notes moaning a minor chord against a major right hand, and pulling stops as if to land a Cessna in a corn field. Thurman the Thumper on the booming bass was muting and popping most notes, except for the ones accidentally sustained, which caused a tingling effect on the hair of my legs. The Marvelous Mario Metronome on the triple-bass electronic drums was obviously a Grand Funk Railroad fan. The combined sound of Tommy Twelve-String, Bubba Bluegrass, Jimmy Jerk-A-Lot and Hot Lick Herbert on guitars brought to mind Willie Nelson and Eddie Van Halen playing dueling guitars to Lester Flatt and Earl Scruggs "Foggy Mountain Breakdown." Last, but not least, was little Tammy-No-Tune on the piercing piccolo.

Then, of course, there were the vocalists: The Holy-Spirit-Led (which way did He go?!) World

Reaction Singers were so graciously led by the worship leader, (If-I-close-my-eyes-they'll-never-see-me) Sammy Sedate. Sammy just happened to be a dead ringer for a male Whoopi Goldberg with two prominent gold fillings in his back upper teeth. Holding it all together from the first row was Sister Ethel and her Tasmanian tambourine, formerly of the Bun-on-the-Head Bunch from Days-Gone-By, Arkansas.

Though the names have all been changed to protect the guilty, I do believe that Nostradamus owes us a great debt, for I'm sure he must have seen this coming in the last days and simply didn't tell us. As I stood there evaluating the situation and trying to maintain some clarity of thought, I just raised my hands, closed my eyes and thanked God they didn't have a steel guitar player.

In the midst of the pandemonium and chaos of flying notes and feedback, God began speaking to me, and I began to understand some things. First, it gradually became obvious to me, "Ah, Majesty, Majesty, Yes, that's it, 'Majesty.' The song they are doing is 'Majesty'!" Secondly, I realized that without a proper understanding of our roles in His presence, musicians sometimes take the position of whoever gets there first, wins. Thirdly, God had finally answered a question that had been in my heart for years: "Where did the word 'Charismaniacs' come from?!"

I know you would undoubtedly like to hear some of the pearls of great wisdom I brought forth to the musicians on Monday night, as well as the

11

godly counsel I gave to the pastor. However, to be quite honest, I can't tell you the rest of the story; it's too depressing. He that hath an undamaged ear, let him hear.

I'm sure there has been a time in all our lives when we have asked the question, "Is God looking at this situation and laughing? Or is He crying?" I believe that in this particular situation, He was laughing. He heard all the bad notes and the many rhythmical and metrical inconsistencies. He saw all the facial contortions and religious gestures being performed in the name of worship. Ridiculous as it may sound, I believe His laughter could be heard throughout heaven. God desires excellence, and musical skill is very important. There is no excuse for musical ignorance or laziness. However, when we take the music of all the different lifestyles, cultures, denominational backgrounds, musical preferences, and educational influences that determine who we are musically, and put them all together into one forty-five-minute explosion on Sunday, I believe what He sees the most are the pure hearts of His children. I think He looks around, laughs, and says, "Hey! Where are my steel guitar players?!"

"Godidic" Worship

I'm sure King David had to deal with some of the same problems in his time. Imagine the task of conducting a four thousand-piece orchestra–complete with all the string, brass, woodwind and percussion sections that we have in today's orchestras. Add to that the task of handling 288 lead singers and thousands of congregational singers. Try keeping all that in order. But David understood the necessity of order for musicians in the House of the Lord. More importantly he understood the importance of releasing a unified sound from the orchestra in which God Himself would dwell.

Years before David began organizing worship in Israel; God established *His* sound in the heart of David. Perhaps as a youth David was just a hairy-legged, redheaded guitar-picker sitting on a flat rock and playing to sheep. He had no political future or prowess. But God saw his heart as he daily worshiped with every ounce of himself. David's love and worship touched the very heart of God to the point that He said, "That boy loves me so much he's after My own heart. Well then, I'll just give him My heart!" The reason God gave David His heart is because He knew David had already given his away. This is still true today. If we really desire to have God's heart, we must give ours away. To the degree that we're willing to give our heart to God, He is willing to give His heart to us. Not only was David a prophet, priest, and king of the nation, he was also the worship leader. Two things dominate the personality of a true worship leader. First, he has a fire in his heart to worship God that will not go out. Secondly, he has the same fire in his heart to see others worship God.

God knew that kings establish standards, so He set David as king over His chosen people to establish the standard of worship for an entire nation. The design for order in what we call Davidic worship is not "Davidic" worship, but "Godidic" worship, for it began in the heart of God (Okay, I know "Godidic" is not a word, but hey, it works). Nevertheless, God deposited His order and sound into the heart of a man raised up as prophet, priest and king.

It is valid to think of David as the scriptural epitome of a musician, but we must understand that music and sound existed before David. God simply used David to bring a concentrated implementation of music and sound to His people. David prophetically focused with song on what God desired to do to and through His people. There are 839 verses in the Word of God that relate to music. Before and after David's time, music was an expression of God. What we typically understand to be music is made up of sound.

Psalm 150 creates the imagery of the heavenly orchestra God designed through David. It is full of various sounds, all pronounced as one voice through the power of praise. It's a listing of the parts which cried out in praise: the trumpet, the harp and lyre, the tambourine, the strings and flute, and the resounding cymbals. David listed these as we would list the parts of our body and call them to attention. "Lift, arm. Walk, leg. See, eyes. Hear, ears." Each instrument of Psalm 150 has a unique function, just like the parts of the body. As Paul says in I Corinthians 12:18, *"God has set the members, each one of them, in the body just as He pleased."* We know Paul is speaking of the church. As a prophet generations before, David understood and used this application of the body to the various elements of sound. All the instruments are needed to operate together, just as all body parts are needed to function properly.

In an orchestra, certain instruments rest while others work. Parts of the body function at different times. For example, when I'm sitting at the table having a conversation with someone, I might use my hands, vocal chords, facial gestures and so on. As I'm elaborating in the conversation, I might stomp my foot on the floor to make a point. The point has been made, and the foot goes back to a rested position. Then my hands might continue to visually accentuate what I'm audibly speaking. Different parts of my body are used within the same conversation.

Applied to musical expression, we discover every member of the orchestral body has its own unique purpose at specific times. In David's orchestra, the trumpets would at times blare to accentuate a particular expression of that Psalm, or drums would be pounded to release a sound of might and fear, or the stringed instruments would be used to paint a picture of peaceful flight. At times there would be the lifting of the hands expressed by the word *yadah*. At times worship would imply kneeling, falling prostrate or dancing with all your might. The instruments became such extensions of the musicians' bodies that as they were called to dance, their instruments would dance with them. Every element of tabernacle worship involved times of work and rest, or for the instruments, tension and release.

David understood the dynamics of musical tension and release. That's why he designated some songs to be accompanied by the flute, stringed instrument or drum, while others specifically called for the clapping of hands. In the body of a song, he would employ a *selah* which would bring emphasis and clarity to the vocabulary of that song. This musical *selah* perfectly matched the lyric, or the prophetic word. This reflected an emotional response expressing God's heart to His people or the people's heart to God. David employed the *selah* to add full impact to what was being spoken. The music would interpret the vocabulary of the song bringing mental imagery through the dynamics of sounds. This instrumentation then caused the lyric to have its greatest impact.

Let's begin this journey into music and sound where it all began—in Genesis.

Chapter Three

The Science of Sound

The day God chose to create light was the day music began. Light and sound travel through the medium of waves. Moving light waves are called electromagnetic waves. The wavelength of an electromagnetic wave determines which type of light it is. As humans, we're only able to see 3 percent of the entire light spectrum, and part of the 97 percent of invisible light is categorized as electromagnetic light. Within electromagnetic light exists a range of wavelengths called radio waves. Within this category of radio waves exists an even smaller range of waves that humans can hear. Essentially, we know that all these categories and forms of light and sound exist within the same spectrum. The first time God said, *"Let there be light,"* (Genesis 1:3). He was also proclaiming the beginning of sound. And He wasn't asking permission for there to be sound. He wasn't in the heavens saying, "Pleeeeaze... *let* there be light" or, "Aw, come on guys... just *let* there be some, you know, light." All He said was, *Or! Or* is the Hebrew root word for light. This was instantaneous creativity of God in action. The thought was said and done. When the voice of God spoke, it became—it was there.

When He said, "light," it was heard in the silent void and darkness. In reality, He was releasing the light of His glory. Remember, the sun and moon were not created until the fourth day, so this light was the light of His glory. In this instant, music was born. Although light and sound are located on different frequencies, they are the same thing. The Bible says, *"God is light, and in Him there is no darkness at all"* (I John 1:5 NAS). Everything that God has ever brought forth has come from His creative voice, the same voice which impregnates the earth with light, sound, music and glory, the elements of God.

The sound of heaven that is called the *"sound of many waters"* (Revelation 14:2 NAS) in the book of Revelation, encompasses all the frequencies in the sound spectrum. The four universal elements are water, wind, fire, and earth. The sound of heaven–all the frequencies of the sound spectrum–can be heard in water, wind, and fire. We are made of the fourth element which is dirt. God desires for that same sound to be heard through the earth. When He created us, He simply animated dirt. Imagine the first sound Adam ever heard was God breathing the wind or the breath of His Spirit.

We are the only ones made in His image. We are the creatures God chose to give free will to accept or reject His sound breathing in us. The wind does not have a will, and neither does fire nor water. Man has been given a will, because man has been given a soul. Therefore, we have a choice to align our sound with the sound of heaven, while the other elements remain inanimate. Fire simply sounds like fire, wind sounds like wind, and water sounds like water. Man sounds like man, but we have been given the creative ability to release the sound of God. The larger the mass of corporate worship we have, the more we sound like a brewing tornado, a blazing forest fire or a raging geyser. So *"let everything that has breath praise the Lord!"* (Psalm 150:6)

Sound is an amazing force. A pair of 30 inch speakers connected to a tone generator can generate a note low enough to literally physically move a building off its foundation. We cannot begin to understand sound until we realize that we are unable to hear most of the sounds that exist. We are continually in the presence of ultrasonic and subsonic sound waves. "Ultra," which means "above," are waves above our threshold of hearing. "Sub," which means "beneath," are waves beneath our threshold of hearing. Just because we don't see the wind does not mean it is not there. Just because we don't hear a sound does not mean it was never made. If a man stands in a forest and speaks, and a woman is not there to correct him, is he still wrong? (Just kidding).

Though I don't recommend anyone trying it because of the physical dangers involved, scientists have experimented and found that by harnessing the energy of an oil well in New Mexico, that they could create an amplifier powerful enough to be heard in Italy. Imagine taking an old Martin guitar, and hammering a D chord, and the sound literally being heard around the world. Most of us walk around unaware of what really surrounds us. We have a great big God who is able to do whatever He wants. He created sound with enough power to cause earthquakes by the sound modulations under the earth's surface. He created sound to be devastating enough to leave nations crumbled to ruins. With awesome earthquakes and mighty continental rumblings, it's amazing to think there is nothing that catches the ear of God more than a simple whisper of praise from the heart of a child.

Sight and Sound

Sound has the power to change everything. Imagine a scene from a movie where a woman is walking down a sidewalk. I'll add some details to spice it up. It's a fall afternoon and the wind is picking up, making the dead leaves swirl around her feet with every step. The street is downtown in a big city. It is crowded with business people on their lunch break. The woman, in her forties, is wearing a navy blue skirt and a white blouse. Her right hand is clutching the strap of her purse, and she is walking extremely fast. From these visuals what do we know about the situation? Very little. We can guess at what the situation might be—maybe she's late for a meeting, maybe she doesn't work and has come downtown to give her husband something at his office. The truth is we know nothing except for what our eyes see. Our eyes simply give us facts.

Now take the same scene and add the eerie sound of a lonely faint chime. Voice this over the background of a futuresque dissonant chord from a synthesizer. Add the boom of a bass drum playing sporadically as if in a death march. Now we feel something. We're concerned for the woman, maybe even scared and on the edge of our seats because we think she's being chased. Change the music to a light piccolo playing over the staccato plucks of an orchestra's violin section and the scene becomes more playful, as if she's running against the heavy flow of people walking the other way. With this background music, she becomes more of an individual heroine whom we're rooting for. Finally, change the music to the slow, lush sound of strings passionately playing "The Love Song" and our hearts drop. Perhaps she is on the way to the hospital where her love lies dying and has only hours to live.

Sound can create a story from dry facts. It stirs our emotions to go beyond facts to feeling. The scene's meaning depends entirely on how the viewer and the listener choose to respond emotionally, and the meaning can also depend on their mood while watching and listening. The revelation that comes to the seer has everything to do with the sounds of the scene.

The woman walking is a picture of the church, progressively taking steps forward, often frantically. The sound being heard as the church goes forward has everything to do with how the seers will interpret what goes on. Therefore, the sound impacts how they will pray, how they will believe, and how they will interpret the activity they see in the church. Is she walking into   a season of peace, a season of joy, or a season of being raped and violated by the world? Music is the indicator. Sound sets the tone of her destiny.

Throughout the generations of history, the spiritual climate of God's people has always had a musical indicator. With every revival, there has been a release of new music or new sound. Whether the music released revival, or whether the revival released the music varies from generation to generation. However, the sound changes as God's people's responses change to what God is doing and saying. I know we could argue that sound and music continually change as a result of the development of the technology of any given generation. But the fact is, God gives the technology also. It's a chicken or egg deal. Any way you look at it, God unveils new songs and new sounds in relationship to the new revelation of His presence in His people. That's why the enemy fights so hard to counterfeit everything that God desires to do musically in a generation.

David was able to impact his generation not only politically, but poetically and prophetically. This prophet, priest, and king brought God into all arenas of life in Israel. As a prophet, He was a worshiping prophet. As a priest, he was a worshiping priest. And as a king, he was a worshiping king. All authority in Israel, whether it is political, ecclesiastical or personal, rested on this man, who was after God's own heart. He established the standards of the day to see, hear, and know God. David, as a worshiper, had committed to performing a vow of worship seven times a day unto God (see Psalm 119:164). Seven times a day, he took his harp and spontaneously sung to God. Those spontaneous expressions of his worship relationship with his God became the lyrics of the nation, and a truth that endures to all generations.

To understand David's lyrics, we must understand how the prophets thought. They thought with a Hebrew mind set, which is often confusing to us, for we typically think with a Greek mind set. When God spoke to the prophets of old, they understood that when God said it, it was done. There was no necessity for working up a lather of faith and motivating themselves to believe that God would do what He said He would do. When God said it, that was enough. In their understanding, God saying it was the same as God doing it. The Hebrew mind, thought intuitively, not philosophically. Their thinking did not coordinate and relate things into a system as the Greek mind does. The Hebrew mind didn't normally think logically. Jesus was not Socrates. There were no shades of meaning and stages of transition in thought, for the Hebrew thought with the eye. Their connection to the prophetic was always optical rather than logical. David saw one thing, then another and the connections between the two visions were not always obvious to the reader. Over the years, Bible scholars have struggled to interpret Scripture in ways the Greek mind can understand. Within one Psalm, the atmosphere and imagery can change a dozen times. Most commentators stumble through the Psalms and are frustrated with the lack of unity in imagery, when in fact David simply sang what he saw, and what he saw was what God was saying. With that in mind, let's see David in the pastoral scene of Psalm 23.

Seeing and Singing

David is sitting on a hillside looking across the green pastures with his harp on his lap, accompanied by thoughts of caring for his sheep. He begins to sing, *"The Lord is my shepherd; I shall not want. He makes me to lie down in green pastures; He leads me beside the still waters. He restores my soul; He leads me in the paths of righteousness for His name's sake"* (Psalm 23:1-3). The images here are a loving shepherd and his sheep lying at rest in green pastures by still waters. Then, in verse four, the imagery is suddenly changed to walking through the valley of the shadow of death: *"Yea, though I walk through the valley of the shadow of death, I will fear no evil; for You are with me; Your rod and Your staff, they comfort me"* (verse 4). Then comes a stumbling block for the commentators, because in the middle of the pastoral scene we're suddenly at an indoor banquet with a table prepared for us. *"You prepare a table before me in the presence of my enemies; You anoint my head with oil; my cup runs over"* (verse 5).

Imagine David sitting on the side of a hill, looking across a meadow at a shepherd and his sheep. Sitting there he sees the shepherd's house, a little black tent made of goat hide. He also sees a fugitive who had just committed murder fleeing across the desert. Chasing him are the avengers of the murder. Though the fugitive is running for his life, if he can only touch the ropes of that tent, he'll be safe, for he knows the laws of hospitality in the desert demand that the shepherd take him in and set the finest table possible before him. The shepherd will then anoint the fugitive's head with oil and give his best provisions as a banquet while the avengers have to stand outside. There's nothing they can do but wait. Inside the shepherd host will serve, bless and anoint him in this place of sanctuary for two days and the intervening night. For that period of time, the fugitive is safe and nothing can touch him except the blessings of his host. When the period of time is over, he must rise, leave the hospice and bear his bloody death.

As the poet David sees this scene, he thinks of the hospitality of God which is without a limit. For in this song, he brings lyric forth as an expression of his life. He could have sung it this way: Though harm and death come to the fugitive that is being followed by the avengers, *"Surely goodness and mercy shall follow me All the days of my life"* (verse 6). And I'll not dwell in the House of the Lord for two days and the intervening night". . . *I will dwell in the house of the Lord forever"* (verse 6).

When we think with the eye, the connection is optical rather than logical. If you see it, sing it. Remember that the Psalms were sung. Not only were they sung, they were accompanied with gestures. In Psalm 36:12 where the words, *"There the workers of iniquity have fallen"* were spoken, I can assure you a finger was pointing as he declared, *"There the workers of iniquity have fallen."* In Psalm 2:4 the psalmist gives us a picture of "God laughing." Gestures and emotions were always a part of the expression of song. The reporter gets the words, but it's the camera that gets the picture.

The eye gate is as important as the ear gate, for unless we see what the Father is doing, how can we hear what He is saying? The foundation of the prophetic song is musically coming into agreement and accompanying what God is doing and saying (see John 5:19). He is now developing our sensitivity to His Spirit through the emphasis on prayer, intercession, praise, and worship, causing His church to walk as a victorious lady in a blue skirt surrounded by songs of deliverance, seeing and hearing with each step the sights and sounds of God's heavenly purpose. May the accompanying soundtrack of this scene impact the world that views us, that they might hear the sound of heaven as we walk with our God.

Chapter Four

Sounds of Shouting, Marching and Rain

Let's look at a few examples of God using sound to accomplish His purposes in man throughout history. Many times in Scripture, God uses strange and bizarre methods to accomplish His purposes. They seldom make sense to the natural mind. But hopefully, found in some of the examples shared, we'll find the ingredients for stretching our faith and unveiling an even greater wonder of God than we've known. In His infinite wisdom, He many times defies logic just to capture our hearts. However, I want to present these stories in such a way that He can also capture our logic and arrest our thinking. Truly His thoughts are higher than our thoughts. That is why unusual tactics such as shouting, marching, and rain were used by God to carry out His will.

Shout!

How many times have we heard the story of Joshua and the city of Jericho and never understood what *really* happened when God's people shouted? First, let's look at the word shout in Scripture. There are more than fifty words used in the Hebrew language in connection with praise. Though they are different words, they are all related. Many of them are derived from the same root word. Praise always requires a body function—clapping, kneeling, singing, etc. One of those words is the word *shabach*, which means "to shout, to address in a loud tone or to commend." It's the most exclamatory form of praise. *Shabach* is translated "praise" four times in the book of Psalms. For instance, Psalm 63:3 says, *"Because Your lovingkindness is better than life, my lips shall praise (shabach or shout) You."* Psalm 117:1 says, *"Praise (shabach* or shout) *Him all you people."* In Psalm 145:4, *"One generation shall praise (shout) Your works to another, and shall declare Your mighty acts."* Psalm 147:12 says, *"Praise* (shout to) *the Lord, O Jerusalem!"* In the Daniel 2:23, we find the corresponding word *shabach* as Daniel shouts his praises to God for giving him wisdom and power.

Note that there is a scriptural principle of shouting the mighty works and acts of God from one generation to another. If a shout can be powerful enough to reach into the next generation, it would behoove us to look deeper into the dynamics and physics of what takes place in the spirit realm when God's people shout. The shout of praise is an exclamatory expression of the heart that's been overwhelmed by God's lovingkindness and greatness. Though more could be said about the shout of praise, let's look instead at another side of this shout. The shout can also be a sound to impact and even devastate the enemy in spiritual warfare.

The first time God identified Himself as the Lord of hosts was with Joshua. In Joshua 5, we find this chosen leader of God laying with his head on a rock, moanin' and groanin', crying, "God, You've called me to take the most fortified city. I can't do it. No way, not me." He was basically in a "Well, I-would-

28

just-throw-myself-at-the-ground-but-I'm-just-afraid-I'd-miss" state of mind. Lying in his poor-me mentality and the grips of depression, a mighty soldier appeared before him, standing with a sword drawn. He was the most fearful-looking sight Joshua had ever seen. Joshua immediately said to him, "You've got to tell me. Are you on *my* side or are you on *their* side?" The warrior looked Joshua in the eye and said, "No. You are on My side. I am the Captain of the hosts. I'm the Commander of the army of the Lord. So that puts *you* on *My* side." And Joshua fell on his face and began to worship. Then he said to him, "What does my Lord want to say to me?" The Captain of the Lord's army replied, *"Take your sandals off your feet, for the place where you stand is holy"* (Joshua 5:15). Joshua immediately did so.

Notice how quickly a state of fear and depression turned into a release of worship, and how quickly a state of worship turned into a release of God's instruction. Not only do we speak to God in worship, but God desires to speak to us. Sometimes the greatest worship is listening. Suddenly Jericho was out of the picture for Joshua. God had his attention. Rather than becoming arrogantly bold to go after Jericho, Joshua simply said, "What does the Lord desire for me to do?" The Captain of the Hosts told him to take off his shoes. Have you ever tried to walk around on the stony terrain of desert mountains barefoot? You'll find that if you walk barefoot across sharp rocks and hard dry ground, you'll walk tenderly. This is a picture of a tender walk in the presence of the Lord. How quickly depression and terror can turn into tenderness and desire when we worship God. From that position, God began to implement His vision through Joshua for releasing the people of God from the oppression of the enemy.

Joshua asked the commander of the Lord's army, "What do you want me to do?" The Captain gave him the strategy: "Listen, you go down there, take seven laps around the wall, give me a big 'Yee-haw' and I'll fold the place." This strategy didn't make sense to the natural mind. Can't you just see Joshua coming back to the people of Israel, saying, "Okay, guys, I've heard from God. This is what we're going to do: We're going to go down there, take seven laps around the city, blow the trumpet, holler a 'Yee-haw' and God's going to do it!" Everybody said, "Right, Joshua." It didn't make sense to their natural minds either. But God was not looking for smarts; He was looking for obedience. Lack of obedience is a major issue with the church today. We have been educated beyond obedience. Smarts and hearts aren't the same thing. He was looking for them to walk in obedience to His Word, no matter what it looked like. It doesn't make sense to the natural mind to bring someone in a church with cancer, rub a little 10W-40 oil on their head, and they walk out healed. Somebody tell me how that works. It's obedience to His Word that works.

In Joshua 6:2-5, we see that Jericho was shut up. In verse two the Lord said to Joshua:

See! I have given Jericho into your hand, its king, and the mighty men of valor. You shall march around the city, all you men of war; you shall go all around the city once. This you shall do six days.

And seven priests shall bear seven trumpets of rams' horns before the ark. But the seventh day you shall march around the city seven times and the priests shall blow the trumpets. Then it shall come to pass, when they make a long blast with the ram's horn, and when you HEAR the SOUND of the trumpet, that all the people shall shout with a great shout; then the wall of the city will fall down flat. And the people shall go up every man straight before him.

Notice that the Lord told Joshua to *"See"* for *"I have given Jericho into your hand"* (verse 2). It was important for Joshua to see as he heard. In verse six he began the process of mobilizing the people of God to obedience, which tells us that he saw what God was saying. God had given the strategy, He had spelled out the tactics and it was time to release the sound of agreement.

In Joshua 6:5 it says, *"When you hear the sound of the trumpet, that ALL the people shall shout with a great shout . . . then the wall of the city will fall down flat."* The people responded out of obedience to God, resulting from Joshua hearing and seeing what the Lord was saying. There was a sound used to implement God's will, and Joshua was required to agree with it. Had they not believed God would do what He said, they certainly would have had no business standing in the face of their enemies tooting their horns and hollering. It took honest-to-goodness mobilized obedience for them to do what they did. As a result of their obeying and releasing the sound, God did what He said He would do.

God instructed them to shout with a great shout. But this was not the *shabach* shout here. This was the word *ruah*, which according to *Strong's* means "to split the ears with sound, as in blowing an alarm or crying out." When they walked in obedience and began to release this earsplitting shout joined with the sound of the shofar and the trumpet blast of prophetic release, the stage for the miraculous was set. The second word for shout used in verse five is not *ruah*, but *truah*. *Truah* is "the clamor or acclamation of the battle cry, especially the clangor of trumpets." This word was prefaced with the words, *"with a great* shout." This was the shout of God.

When God's people shouted out of obedience, God got involved and shouted too. As a unit, they took the city. God's Word had come to pass according to verse two: *"See! I have given Jericho into your hand."* God did what He said He would do. When they walked in obedience and released a battle cry by faith, God's voice joined the sound. I propose that was more miraculous than meets the eye. Think of it. Jericho was fortified with a double wall. The outer wall was six feet thick and the inner wall was twelve feet thick. The two walls were fifteen feet apart, and this space of separation was sometimes packed with sand and stone. So basically, Joshua's men faced a wall thirty-three feet wide and thirty feet high. If a wall of that size fell, an army still couldn't get over the rubble. There would be just a big pile of rocks. But in response to the shout, the hand of God telescoped the wall into the ground and the Israelites walked across on flat ground. When God joins the shout of His people, spiritual walls will fall.

Shout for the Presence

After a loss of four thousand Israelite soldiers at the hands of the Philistines, the elders of Israel realized their desperate need for the presence of God (see I Samuel 4:3). They said, *"Let us bring the ark of the covenant of the Lord from Shiloh to us, that when it comes among us it may save us from the hand of our enemies."* So they went to Shiloh to retrieve the Ark of the Covenant which was also with Joshua at Jericho. When the ark entered the camp, all Israel shouted *(ruah)* with a great shout *(truah)* so that the earth rang (verse 5). The last time the *ruah* and *truah* came forth, the earth trembled and quaked and the walls of Jericho fell. This time when the shout came, the earth rang. When the Philistines heard the noise of the shout, they understood God had come to battle on behalf of Israel. The Philistines cried, *"Woe to us! Who will deliver us from the hand of these mighty gods? These are the gods who struck the Egyptians with all the plagues in the wilderness"* (verse 8). They knew the awesome power of God. The Philistines said to one another, "We don't want to be slaves of these Hebrews, so let's get out there and fight like men." The Philistines fought and killed 30,000 of Israel's footman that day. The ark of God was taken and Israel lost a great battle.

Presumption Brings Defeat

You might say, "Wait a minute! The Ark of the Covenant was there just like Jericho! The shout took place just like Jericho! It was God's people, just like the battle of Jericho! What was the difference?" The difference was that Hophni and Phinehas, the rebellious sons of the priest Eli, had stolen the Ark of the Covenant and brought it into battle to be used as a trump card. There was not an obedient bone in their bodies. Yes, the shout sowed fear into the minds and hearts of the enemy, but the fear only motivated them to fight even harder against the Israelites. This was not God's strategy; therefore, God did not honor it. God refused to be reduced to a formula. He's not a formula; He's a Father.

Whether it is a shout of praise, warfare, or presumption, there can be great spiritual power in the shout. If you've ever been to a football stadium or a concert, you know how impacting it can be standing in the midst of 80,000 people shouting with aggression. A shout for a shout's sake can be very motivating, but its effect is only temporary. Imagine you're now in the same stadium filled with 80,000 who walk humbly with God and wholeheartedly embrace His strategy in spiritual warfare. As they shout, it's out of obedience to His eternal purposes. They shout to bring forth His power and grace. Needless to say, there's nothing temporary about the effect of that shout.

There are many other instances of the shout in Scripture and a variety of Hebrew words that are translated "shout," which I won't take time to address here. But I want to clarify that there is a definite distinction between the shout of praise you find in the book of Psalms and the shout that releases God's power, as seen in the book of Joshua. One incites praise *to* the Father, while the other invokes the power of the Father. Both require humility and obedience to be effective. The key is to rise up out of depression and fear as Joshua did and behold the Captain of the Hosts. The host of the Lord is a myriad of heavenly warriors–an army with the power of heaven and the strength of their awesome God to war with you, not against you. In other words, when we shout, we don't shout alone. The shout of God is an awesome thing.

The Sound of Marching

Another example of God using sound to accomplish His purposes through man is found in II Samuel 5. In verse 18, the Philistines had come against David. In verse 19, *"And David inquired of the Lord, saying, 'Shall I go up against the Philistines? Will you deliver them into my hand?' And the Lord said to David, 'Go up, for I will doubtless deliver the Philistines into your hand.'"* So David smote the Philistines and said, *"The Lord has broken through my enemies before me, like a breakthrough of water"* (verse 20). Then he took their idols and their images and burned them.

Later, the Philistines came up against David again. Knowing that the Lord had anointed him to overcome the Philistines, David could have simply gone out and fought them. But he didn't presume a victory. He inquired of the Lord again. This time the Lord surprisingly said, *"You shall not go up; circle around behind them, and come upon them in front of the mulberry trees. And it shall be, when you hear the sound of marching in the tops of the mulberry trees, then you shall advance quickly"* (II Samuel 5:23-24).

The sound of marching indicated to David that the Lord had gone out to strike the camp of the Philistines.

The sound of marching in the tops of the mulberry trees was the sound of the heavenly host of warriors fighting on David's behalf. Again, there was a sound involved. After their enemies had been overcome, David and the Israelites brought up the ark of the Lord with shouting and with the sound of the trumpet. I'll bet the sound of those voices and trumpets' blasting wasn't too different from what the enemy heard on the tops of the mulberry trees.

The Sound of Rain

The shout of God and the sound of marching that David and Joshua heard came at desperate times. Both men were in war, needing a miracle to overcome their enemies. However, in the Old Testament, the sound of heaven wasn't exclusively heard in war times. God demonstrated His power through Elijah in I Kings 18, as the prophet called down fire from heaven. As fire from heaven consumed the sacrifice, all the people fell on their faces and began to worship God. When three years of famine passed, Elijah told the Israelite king, Ahab, to rise up, eat and drink, for he had heard in his spirit a *"sound of an abundance of rain"* (I Kings 18:4). Immediately, Elijah went to the top of Mount Carmel and cast himself to the earth with his face between his knees in a travailing or birthing position. Elijah told his servant to go look toward the sea. The servant looked and saw nothing. Elijah told him to go and look for rain seven times.

On the seventh time, he said, *"Behold, there ariseth a little cloud out of the sea, like a man's hand"* (verse 44 KJV). Notice this happened on the seventh time. With Joshua seven laps were required with seven trumpets to take Jericho. Throughout Scripture, seven is understood to be the number of completion or perfection. At the completion of your obedience you will find the completion of God's will.

Elijah told his servant to go tell Ahab to get his chariot harnessed up, because rain was coming. Soon the heavens became black with clouds and wind, and there was a great rain. Notice in verse 41 that Elijah *heard* the *"sound of an abundance of rain,"* which brought him to a place of intense prayer and travail. In verse 44, his servant declared that he could *see* a cloud. There was a *hearing* and a *seeing* of the coming rain. Then a manifestation of clouds, wind and a great rain occurred. I think it would be safe to say that if Elijah had not heard the sound, and come into agreement with what he heard, and declared accordingly, he would not have seen the rain. Just as David had seen and brought forth the hearing (see Psalm 23), we see that Elijah heard and brought forth the seeing. When we align ourselves with the prophetic hearing and seeing that God is unveiling today, I believe it will bring a whole new understanding to the New Testament Scripture, *"Eye has not seen, nor ear heard, nor have entered into the heart of man the things which God has prepared for those who love Him"* (I Corinthians 2:9).

The Sound of Chariots and Horses

Elisha experienced the supernatural sound of heaven in the form of thundering horses and chariots. In II Kings 6, the king of Syria was warring against Israel. The king took council with his servants and told them where he was going to place his camp. Elisha told the king of Israel to avoid passing the place where the Syrians were. Needless to say, the king of Syria was very angry at Elisha for warning the king of Israel. The king of Syria sent his spies out with a great host of chariots, horses and soldiers to abduct Elisha. Afraid, Elisha's servant said to him, *"What shall we do?"(Verse 15)* He told his servant not to fear *"For those who are with us are more than those who are with them"* (verse 16). Realizing this did not calm his servant's fears, Elisha prayed and said, *"Lord, I pray, open his eyes that he may see"* (verse 17). The Lord opened the young man's eyes, and he saw in the spirit that the mountain was full of horses and chariots of fire all around Elisha. God opened the spirit realm according to Elisha's prayer. What would it do for our faith if we had a lifestyle of prayer and prophetic insight into the spirit realm? What if we could see not only our enemies but the heavenly warriors given to us for the purpose of spiritual warfare? In the natural, the young man saw Syrian soldiers. After Elisha prayed the servant's spiritual eyes were opened to see the heavenly warriors there to war on behalf of the man of God. What would just one experience of being able to see with spiritual eyes do to us?

In the same chapter, Samaria is surrounded by the Syrians. There was a famine so great in Samaria that people were selling a donkey head for eighty pieces of silver and dove's dung for five pieces. The famine was so horrendous that some were literally eating their own children. In II Kings 7:1, Elisha stood and said, *"HEAR the word of the Lord. Thus says the Lord: Tomorrow about this time, a seah of fine flour shall be sold for a shekel and two seahs of barley for a shekel"* (II Kings 7: 1). Right in the middle of total devastation and depravity, Elisha prophesied the bizarre. Within 24 hours, everything was going to be different. One of the king's men in a sarcastic tone said, "Well I guess, maybe if the Lord opens the windows of heaven." Elisha's response to his unbelief was, "You're going to see it with your eyes, but you will not eat a bite of it" (verse 2). In the meantime four outcasts sat outside the gate of the city—four leprous men who had not heard the prophet.

Some years ago, I had the privilege of ministering in a leper colony seventy miles off the Black Sea in southern Russia. I spent an afternoon in a room with about seventy-five lepers. To see the impact of that disease on a physical body is astounding. I saw people without ears, eyes, noses or fingers, and many or most of them had at least one limb missing as a result of this horrible disease. Nevertheless, they were some of the most wonderful people I'd ever met in my life. As they shared their life stories and I shared mine, there was an instant bond of friendship. I could hardly believe some of them had spent as many as fifty years sitting in this room every day. I was one of the first Americans they had ever seen. Their stories greatly impacted me. I will take many of their stories and acts of kindness with me throughout my life. As I prepared to leave after two and a half hours of conversation, an old Russian leper stood on the only leg he had left and with a smile on his face, said, "Young man, an old Russian proverb says that one old friend is better than two new ones. So please come again, because now you are our old friend." As touched and exhilarated as I was by that encounter, the reality is that people in that condition do not have much to look forward to, since their bodies are daily being weakened by the cursed disease. Having experienced the hopelessness of these people gave me an idea of what was going on in the hearts and minds of these four leprous men sitting at the gate of Samaria.

Perhaps one of the lepers looked at the other and said, "What are our choices? If we go into the city, we'll just die like all the rest. If we just sit here, we'll eventually die of leprosy. Our other choice is to get up and walk into the camp of the enemy. Then they will do one of two things: they will either kill us or feed us. If they spare us, we live. If they kill us, we die." So they rose early the next morning and walked into the camp of the Syrians. When they got there, nobody was home. What had happened? These four little eighty-pound, eyeless, ear-less, nose-less lepers with possibly five feet between them and two arms in the crowd, shuffled and dragged their wretched little bodies along the road. As they went, God caused their footsteps to be heard in the ears of their enemy as the noise of thousands of chariots, thousands of horses, and the noise of a great host. The enemy thought Israel must have hired the massive armies of the Hittites and the Egyptians to fight them. So they jumped up and ran for their lives when they heard *"the noise of horses—the noise of a great army"* (II Kings 7:6) coming down on them. Pandemonium and chaos swept over the entire camp.

But it was nothing more than four little wilted-away lepers. All because Elisha said, *"Hear the word of the Lord"* (I Kings 7:1). The enemy fled their camp in fear of their own lives and left all of their food, drink, silver, gold, and raiment. When the news came back to the city, the king and his assistant still couldn't believe it. There was such a stampede as the food was being brought in the gates that the sarcastic king's assistant was trampled under feet. This fulfilled what the prophet had told him: *"you shall see it with your eyes, but you shall not eat of it"* (verse 2).

This story provides a vivid picture of the greatness of our God and His ability to bring His word to pass. Do you think in the natural that there is any possibility those four leprous men's withered limbs dragging along the road made the sound that was heard? No. But I do believe the horses and chariots of fire that Elisha had seen earlier had a part in all of this. That was the bunch making the noise. If our spiritual prophetic eyes are opened as Elisha's servant's eyes were opened, we will be able to see how God can accomplish His Word. A sound was used by God to free the people from famine, poverty, depression, oppression, and ungodly authority (for the king died in the gates as well). All this happened within twenty-four hours.

Chapter Five

Early American Sound

When this nation began, it didn't inherently have music simply because it was a newborn nation. At least five European countries–Spain, England, France, Holland and Sweden–sent ships across the Atlantic ocean to make settlements in the land we know today as the United States. These ships brought people with their own individual customs, habits and ideas, which formed the culture of this new nation. No doubt some of them brought their sailor songs while others brought their traditional sounds. There weren't a significant number of musical instruments of any kind during those times because cargo space was too precious to waste on musical gear. However, the old hymns of praise sung in their homelands and lullabies that lulled their babies to sleep certainly became a part of the new communities.

In some of the countries, music played a more important role than in others. But the only kind of music the Pilgrims and Puritans brought with them to this country were the psalms they had sung in England. There were only eight melodies or tunes, and the ability to sing these tunes constituted the colonists' entire knowledge of music. There were no instruments to speak of in their culture, and instruments were certainly not used during worship.

Imagine a Sunday church service in New England in colonial times. At 9:00 a.m. people were called to church by the sound of a conch shell, a trumpet, or the roll of a drum. The long service was broken up by the singing of songs. A deacon, elder or minister acted as the song leader. At times they would even gather their pitch for leading the a cappella songs by pecking on a candle holder. There were few songbooks, if any, and most of the congregation couldn't have read them if they had them. As a result, the songs were sung by a method called lining. The leader would sing one line, and the congregation would repeat it, and so on. Can you imagine what it must have been like the day they sang the 119th Psalm? If the leader had a good ear or good pitch, the singing would be musical. But if the leader couldn't carry a tune in a bucket or if he pitched the song too high or too low, the sound hardly resembled music. With all the different accents and pronunciations, sometimes it was nothing more than a loud noise. At times, it must have taken at least an hour to get through a Psalm—but it was a beginning.

The New Englanders were dead-set against music as a means of pleasure. While they had lived in England, they objected to such pleasures as plays, dancing and music—particularly instrumental music. Musical instruments were considered to be instruments of the devil. These colonists found reasons in the Bible for many of their beliefs. For example, Amos 5:23 says, *"I will not hear the melody of your stringed instruments."* This was interpreted to

43

mean that instrumental music was improper. Some of the colonists of the day did not even believe in the singing of songs. They justified that by the passage in the New Testament that says a Christian should make melody only *"in his heart"* (Ephesians 5:19). One group opposed any kind of singing or music. There were heated discussions about how singing should be done among those who embraced singing. Some of the questions most frequently raised were: Should one person sing for the whole congregation, the others joining in only to sing "Amen," or should the whole congregation sing? Should women be allowed to sing or only men? Should carnal men and pagans be permitted to sing or only Christians and church members? Should it be lawful to sing songs and tunes invented by men or should the congregation sing as inspired?

One group determined that singing was the sole right of Christians. Heathen Indians were given only the privilege of saying "Amen" at the end of the song. This group also said that women could not sing or utter an "Amen" at the end of the song. Others believed that to sing a melody composed or made by a man was only a vain show. They believed God would not be pleased with the praise in which man had created the melody. Others considered the hymn tunes by many to be as sacred as the words themselves.

The preface to the songbooks published in England, from which their songs were taken, gives us an idea of the direction the Christian colonists followed in singing. The psalms of tribulation were to be sung "with a low voice and in long measure." The psalms of thanksgiving were to be sung with an "indifferent voice, neither too loud nor too slow." The psalms of rejoicing were to be sung "with a loud voice and in swift measure."

The Jamestown colonists arrived several years before the Puritans and Pilgrims, but left no record of music. We know little of the music of any of the southern colonists who were in America during the first hundred years. It seems likely, however, that these early settlers must have enjoyed music a little more than the Northern colonists. These early settlers whistled and hummed at their work, sang at their church services, and did not have all the religious objections to singing and instruments that the New Englanders had. By the late 1600s, in Williamsburg, Virginia, there were concerts and plays, complete with gentlemen and their ladies in velvet, dancing to stately minuets and Virginia reels. Music in the North, however, maintained a primitive, stoic attitude with no freedom in rhythms or melodies.

The Sound of the Storm

Our musical heritage continued through the Triangular Slave Trade. English ship owners traveled to the west coast of Africa to capture slaves, then crossed the Atlantic to America, and sailed back again to England. Their journey formed a triangular pattern and was thus named the Triangular Slave Trade. America, the new "land of the free, and home of the brave," had such a high demand for slaves that some of these slave-ship owners had to provide as many as three thousand slaves per year just to make their quota and stay in good standing with the British government. Later, history revealed that many of the African jungle tribe leaders wanted to get in on the action and profit. Some tribal leaders intentionally created war situations between tribes in the same culture. At that time, it was justifiable to capture another tribe or nation and bring them into slavery during war times. As the chiefs captured other tribes, they would sell them to the British as slaves. Through selling their rivals to slave traders, they were able to create a better economy for themselves by receiving goods such as iron, metals, and other things they didn't have.

In the middle of this greed and commerce, the victims were the tribes, overcome by their oppressors. They fought for their lives using their instruments for spiritual warfare to call on their gods. Many African tribes had no lyric in their music, only rhythm, harmony, and various tones. They spiritually used these elements, without vocabulary, to call upon the gods to bring storms. The traditions of some pagan rituals such as Voodoo dolls and pagan ceremonies emerged this way. They would axe out the heads of gargoyle-looking things and stick them in trees. Initially they were put there to ward off the evil spirits working to take them into slavery. Through these and other rituals, they called upon the gods of the sun, moon, stars, fire, river, mountains, thunder, sea, wind, love, and death. They beckoned these gods to bring tornadoes, hurricanes, fires, and other violent weather to the west coast of Africa. They wanted the storms to hinder English ships from coming into port to capture them.

During every season of bad weather the tribes were at peace. They believed they were using their music to call up these storms. When they heard the sound of storms–the sound of the rushing wind, water and rain–they knew it represented peace for them and they would not be brought into slavery and oppression. Their physical condition and spiritual climate were directly related to what they believed they were conjuring up through their music. Then suddenly a season would come with a gentle southerly breeze blowing, and they would come under panic and fear. They moved their camp because they knew the peaceful, calm seasons were the very seasons in which they could be destroyed and taken into slavery.

In that era, the English captured slaves by the thousands. One of the most notorious of all the slave-traders was John Newton. He had even been taken as a slave once himself. After he gave his heart to the Lord, he scripted the words to "Amazing Grace" out of the guilt and shame of his slave trading. As the quickening of the Holy Spirit brought truth to his life, he wrote:

> Amazing grace, how sweet the sound
> That saved a wretch like me
> I once was lost, but now am found
> Was blind, but now I see

He realized that he had been wrongly blinded to the injustice of slavery. "Amazing Grace" became an expression of an entire people and still is today. It is the song most frequently sung in black churches across America. Talk about the redemptive purposes of God! Repentance is the right action. God wants to bring a nation to repentance that has had generations of wrong responses to sin and violation against one another. Warring in the spirit realm musically is important as musical styles are restored.

The white wealthy plantation owners, who justified slavery biblically because there were slaves in the Bible, were proud to have slaves doing all their work and making money for them. Some slave holders even thought of the African Americans as "animals without souls." To these slave holders, the African slaves were considered just an animal out of a jungle somewhere. Understand this attitude was not true in every case. There are many accounts of slave holders and slaves who had true friendships and acts of kindness between them—as kind as it could possibly be and still be called slavery. Nevertheless, many slave holders realized the black man's talent for making sounds to entertain them. The slaves sang harmonies the whites had never heard before. The Africans' musical DNA brought rhythm, harmony and the natural ability to hear harmonies to America. At that time, harmony wasn't allowed in the church in America because it was thought to bring attention to man rather than God. Choirs weren't allowed in churches because they were believed to be a display of talent. Music schools didn't exist. There were no professional musicians. Music was not a priority of the day for the white man, though it played a stronger role in the lives of his ancestors. He didn't have time for music. He was trying to build a country.

The slaves of the southern plantations began to sing a song the white man had never heard before.

The slave holders used the blacks for their own entertainment. They were called "coon singers" because they would sit out in the dark at night singing their strange harmonies, with only the whites of their eyes shining in the dark. It was an eerie, wonderful sound that provided entertainment—their television or radio of the day, if you will.

A few of the white folks became fond of their slaves because they were so entertained by their rhythm and dance. The slaves' music had all the things that the white man's music lacked. The white churches' music consisted of opening up the Psalter and singing in a drone:

> My God, my God why has thou forsaken me?
> (My God, my God why has thou forsaken me?)
> Oh God, my God I cry in the daytime.
> (Oh God, my God I cry in the daytime)

Songs of Deliverance

The slaves didn't even know how to spell "harmony," but they had it in them. The white slave holders were so entertained by their singing that they didn't allow slaves to talk while working in the fields, but forced them to sing. The white man designated a single line-boss to set the tempo for the work of the day. This was often an elderly black man chosen by the white owner. As they worked the cotton fields, the line-boss started them by singing, "When the big rivah meet the little rivah." All the slaves, called "darkies," replied, "Follow the drinkin' gourd." The line-boss led, "And when the sun shine on the other side of the

49

mountain." Follow the drinkin' gourd. "And when the wind come and meet your face." Follow the drinkin' gourd.

They sang this song in an antiphonal response, also called "lining," which is the same way David and the Israelites, the Puritan settlers, and other people groups sang. Because most of the workers were uneducated, the Scriptures were learned through antiphonal response singing. In this way, they musically came into agreement with the Word of God, or the prophetic word of the lead singer. The reality of that spiritual release became a part of them. Through song they were confessing what the prophet of the Lord sang. Now the white man, in his "superior intelligence," didn't know what was going on. The slaves were actually singing the map to the Underground Railroad. The "drinking gourd" referred to the Big Dipper. The lyrics covertly told them to follow the Big Dipper when they came to where the two rivers met. The lyrics "when the sun shine" indicated that escaping slaves were to rest during the day and travel at night.

The entire Underground Railroad, their pathway to freedom, was mapped out in song. David would have called this a song of deliverance. An entire race of people taught and admonished one another with songs, hymns and spiritual spontaneous songs (*ode pneumaticos* in Greek). These spiritual songs were sown into their very being. They knew the path to freedom as well as they knew their own names. These were true songs of deliverance. There were various versions of the song, depending on where you were located. Escaping from the Delta, for instance, required a different route than escaping from the North Georgia Mountains. Whatever the case, each slave planted the lyrics to these songs–which could sometimes contain dozens of verses–deep within their heart. Just as David spoke of hiding the Word of God in one's heart, these slaves hid the pathway to freedom in their hearts.

How could they memorize all the lyrics? First, these songs were the only communication the slaves had with one another all during the day of work. For ten hours, they would be in the cotton fields repeating the songs over and over again, making sure everyone knew every word to each verse. They weren't just memorizing the words, they were planting and nurturing these words of hope and life in the core of their beings. Secondly, realize their very lives depended on remembering these words. Think about it. If your chance to freedom, and the freedom of your family's next five generations, was dependent upon you remembering the words of this song, you would memorize each word, whatever the cost.

Spirituals and Shouts

Meanwhile, some of the white men made a big mistake–they started loving these people and took a few of them to church, especially in Kentucky. Black churches began to spring up everywhere because there was less oppression in Kentucky than in the deep South. Suddenly all these black folks started getting saved right and left and God was pouring out His Spirit on them. However, some of the white folks eventually realized strength was emerging from this, and they brought the blacks back into harsher submission.

The black man had two kinds of expressions for worship. First they had the spirituals. As they sang spirituals, they sat on old benches and rocked back and forth. Their bodies had to say what their spirits were saying. They got involved in the music—body, soul, and spirit. If you're going to sing it, you've got to feel it. If you don't feel it, it's not even real. The second expression was the shouts. They brought the same exuberance that was natural to their rhythms in the African jungles into the kingdom of God. They birthed what the Pentecostal movement later called "Jericho marches." It was a natural part of their worship. When those shouts would start in the service, they had an old deacon who would stand there and make sure nobody lifted their feet off the floor as they shuffled around the room. They superstitiously believed if their feet came off the floor they might trip over the cross and go to hell. They would also bring a big cauldron and turn it upside down in the middle of the floor because they believed the cauldron would capture their sounds to keep the boss man from hearing it. The cauldron would hold the sound so they wouldn't be beaten and whipped by the slave-owners. It was another African superstition taken from the Voodoo tradition. But God honored it and it worked.

As the people circled the room in these "shouts," there was always one person in the group that could read, typically a woman who worked in the "big house" with access to books. From Psalm 21 she would say, *"The King shall joy in thy salvation."* Then everyone would sing the line together, repeating after her. It was like tag-team preaching. Again, it was antiphonal response. It was a declaration of freedom coming through the Word of God. As soon as it was taken in, it would be declared by the people.

The instrumentation of the "shouts" consisted of a stick about the size of a broomstick. An old man called the "stick man" would set the tempo for each song by tapping the stick. As he would hammer out a rhythm on the floor accompanied by hand-clapping and foot-tapping, all the melodies and harmonies would combine a call-and-response type of singing. The words and music blended to release a sound perfectly responding to what the leader declared.

One thing God wants to release prophetically now is a reality of our authority. As soon as the Word of God comes, we are to have the authority in God and the integrity of the Holy Spirit to release the Word. We must release the Word, not letting it get caught in the spiritual battlefield of our minds keeping us in bondage generation after generation, afraid of the reality of God coming forth in us. Instruments will be involved in this prophetic release. As soon as the instrument strikes, healing will take place and bondage will be broken. As soon as the word is verbalized, release will come. It will be just like the prophets of old. When God declares it, that means He will do it. It's not a matter of working up a spiritual lather of faith and moving in presumption and manipulation. It's a matter of agreeing with the Word, and becoming the action of the Word.

At times, the slaves would sing a song called "Jubilee." The lyric was, "Shout, my children, 'cause yo free." They were singing and shouting their freedom before the Emancipation Proclamation. They proclaimed it before Lincoln ever penned it. In that sense it was a prophetic song.

The Sound of Slavery

The songs of the slaves weren't written neatly on paper, nor were they composed one Sunday while sitting in a nice church pew. These songs were born with the same elements of a natural birth–blood, sweat, and tears. As part of oral tradition, they were passed down from generation to generation. Perhaps old Aunt Hattie would lie in the middle of the night in a slave camp in upper North Carolina. She would be thinking about the preaching and dancing that had taken place, and the prayers that had been said that day in the "meetin' house." One prayer recorded from these churches was from a slave preacher who said:

"O mah God an'mah Father, ain't you see how disgroun' do trimble same like judgement day? Come down hyuh, Lawd, an' help po' people in dere trial and tribbilation, but o, do Mass Gawd, be sho' an' come yo'self an' doansen' Yo' Son, because disain' no time for chillun..."

That was straight from his heart–from a real man to a real God. His theologies were a little sideways, but all of our theologies have been a little sideways at times. We've all walked in the light we've had. Now we're walking in a time when the light's coming on.

But old Aunt Hattie would lay there in a soft, low, groan-of-a-tone, and sing, "Mmm." In those shanty shacks with paper-thin walls, everyone would hear it when old Aunt Hattie started to sing. She would sing "Mmm" and all of the others would wake up and sing back to her: "Mmm." She would do it again, as they would. And then she would start to remember what the old preacher had preached that night, and she would sing, "We are... " They knew to repeat her: *We are . . .* She'd take a switch to them the next day if they didn't. "Climbin'... " *Climbin'.* "Jacob's... " *Jacob's.* "Ladder... " *Ladder.* "We are... " *We are...* "Climbin'" *Climbin'.* "Jacob's... " *Jacob's.* "Ladder... ." *Ladder.* And the song would begin swirling around in a round. Whatever she said, they would sing, and the whole thing would become a song. Traditionally it became part of their culture, that responsive sound and soul to the black music.

The Blues Were Born Black

There was a well-educated woman named Charlotte Forten who was born in the North and brought South to Edisto Island, South Carolina. She was a brilliant, young black teacher and poet. Not long after she arrived in South Carolina, in the middle of the night she heard the sounds of screaming from a young man being flogged in the quarters by slave owners. It gripped her heart because she had never experienced anything like that before. She only knew of it from a distance. It had such an impact on her that before light broke the next morning, after being awake all night tormented by the sounds of the beating, she began writing to express the depths of hurt and pain. The only way she knew to express it was poetically, using the color blue to depict her state of mind. Obviously, expressing herself through her poetry brought some relief. But for those like this young man who did not have the education to write or reason away their anguish, she wondered how they dealt with their hurt and pain. She later asked the young man, to which he replied, with his back still shredded, "Ma'am, I sings it away." Nothing could take the song away from him. As long as he had a song, he had a future.

Charlotte Forten wrote poems that were distributed throughout the South under another name so readers wouldn't know it was "just some black woman." Her poems went throughout the South and into the Delta, where a line from a poem in which she wrote about "the blue night" became a coined phrase for the oppressed, poor, destitute lives of the slaves. It became the word that was planted upon a musical style called the "blues."

The musical styles of the blues and jazz are siblings. The first jazz group in America was called "Stale Bread and the Spasms," a group of young men from New Orleans. They took all the inherited expressions of music they had learned from their slave parents and had sung in church, and formed an entirely new style of sound. But it always reverted back to the roots. Old Aunt Hattie would take the "lead" in singing, and everyone else would become the band, although it was all vocal. These men took the sounds, and once they had instruments, created jazz out of the very same expression sown into them by their parents. As these new styles made their way up and across the Delta, they planted seeds that were later harvested as the Memphis blues and the St. Louis blues. In St. Louis, the blues were transformed by W.C. Handy into the St. Louis blues. As the people and music continually made their way to different parts of the culture, this evolved into the Chicago blues.

A combination of the blues and jazz styles even made its way into the Pentecostal churches. The sound became so raw and rugged that it formed the musical foundation for the Pentecostal sound. The sound continued to evolve, until out of the Assemblies of God sound (which influenced people like Elvis Presley, Jerry Lee Lewis, and Carl Perkins), rock music was born. From the combination of the Pentecostal church sound and the juke joints of the Delta came the world's most revolutionary music, "rock 'n' roll."

Raw and Rugged's OK

Today the sound continues to evolve. In the cross-pollination of all these other music styles, I believe God says, "Listen guys, go ahead and do whatever you want to for all the purposes you desire that are gratifying to your flesh—I'm still going to win this thing in the end. I'm still going to bring it all back home where it belongs. It's going to be a rugged, raw sound. It's going to have some kick and bite to it. It's going to have times of tenderness to it. It's going to have times of stillness and intimacy to it, and times of growling, kicking, snorting, and shouting to it. It's going to have all those things, and they're all going to be combined into one sound that will be heard in thanksgiving and praise unto Me."

The evolution of a sound, which encompasses rhythm, melody, and harmony, with all the emotional and physical responses the sound evokes, can be used to mold and shape the belief systems of man. The sound can either deposit faith in God or rebellion towards God causing a positive or negative impact on an entire generation. When four kids from Liverpool, influenced by the fathers of rock 'n' roll, can hypnotize the nations using their unique expression of sound, we must agree it's a powerful force. The powerful force of the Beatles gave millions of people a united vocabulary and expression.

Our vocabulary is groomed throughout all the days of our lives by the impact our music has on us. Our state songs reflect this. For example, Tennessee has a state song of betrayal. The song of a lover being lost to a best friend is called the "Tennessee Waltz." I don't believe there has ever been a more beautiful melody penned by any writer or composer. But in its beauty, it talks about hurt, wounding and betrayal. And we wonder why Tennessee has one of the highest divorce rates in all of America. It has to do with our belief system, which is directly related to what is being sung and released over the land on a continual, daily basis.

I want to know something. Where are the congregations that will release the song with the Holy Spirit's power and dynamics to change the belief systems of a nation and declare that abortion, sexual abuse, drugs, and murders are abominations before God? If we really believe what we say we believe, where's the grit to release it and get something done? I believe God is putting spiritual cannons in churches across the nation that will release His power in song. His power is released through song as we have the same vocabulary, at the same time, with the same rhythm and melody unto the same Lord. If we bring a united expression from our diversity of musical styles and preferences, whether it is rock, bluegrass, jazz, blues, classical or gospel, we will see God go to war on our behalf. If we can lift up our voices and instruments to make one united sound, whether it is the sound of the wind of the Spirit, the fire of the Spirit, or the shout or the whisper, He will wreak havoc and destruction on the camps of our enemies. These are the enemies that have provoked mankind to hate, abuse, oppress, and violate one another. He will break the chains of bondage over those who have become slaves to sin. May God once again sound His song of deliverance into all our hearts that says, "Follow the drinkin' gourd."

Chapter Six

Water & Thunder

Revelation 19:6 refers to the *"sound of many waters" and of "mighty thunderings."* That's the sound of corporate worship in heaven. For us to understand what that sounds like, think of 10,000 Niagara Falls. Think of 250,000 people in the Super Dome, multiplied 250,000 times and every person releasing every ounce of their energy, body, soul, and spirit in an explosive expression of worship unto God. It sounds like white noise, or the sound of many waters. The fact is, that's what it sounds like in heaven. That sound in heaven is an awesome force that comes straight from the throne.

As humans, God created us with the ability to hear between 16 and 16,000 hertz. That is 16 vibrations per second up to 16,000 vibrations per second. When I hit an "A" note on the piano, your eardrum vibrates 440 times per second. That's what makes it an "A" note. When you go up a note, your eardrum vibrates more times per second. When you go down a note, it vibrates fewer times per second.

If the entire sound spectrum were represented by a graph, three feet wide, humans could only hear three-fourths of an inch of the entire spectrum. There's a huge portion of sound that we never hear because it's either above or below the human audio threshold. It's like a dog whistle. When we blow a dog whistle, we don't hear it. But a dog goes totally silly over the thing because his hearing is created a little differently than ours. We hear only three-fourths of an inch of that three-foot graph.

An oscilloscope is a device created to detect and determine sound frequencies. If you set an oscilloscope beside Niagara Falls, it will go off both ends at the same time. There are sounds within the sound of the falls that are beyond what an oscilloscope can measure. Our invented devices to capture the unheard and unseen things on earth are limited. In heaven, however, there are no limitations. There, twenty-four hours a day, the sound of many waters rolls from the throne and into the throne room.

Dedicating Tikes and Temples

When the sound of many waters, which is the song of the Lord, comes illuminating out of heaven and joins the realm that we are living in, phenomenal things happen. Take a look at the shepherds on the night Jesus was born. Just imagine you're a shepherd in those back fields of Israel. I've got to tell you, there's not much that goes on during the nightshift in the sheep-herding business. Every now and then you'll hear a little old "baa." The rest of the time, well, it's sort of laid back.

You're standing out there at 3:00 a.m., recollecting the four wonderful "baas" you've heard during the night, when all of a sudden the angel of the Lord appears, a massive blast of light shines around you and out of heaven this multitude of angelic voices start singing, "Hallelujah." Think about that. A couple of minutes ago, you were waiting on a "baa," and now all of a sudden, all of heaven is lit up and there's the sound of many waters and the sound of thunder. The sound of heaven has come to earth. And it's just announcing this little baby being born. Now that's some baby dedication service!

This same sound had been heard earlier on earth. Actually, it was right in the middle of another dedication service, as told in II Chronicles 5:11-14. Only this time it was the dedication of the resting place for the ark of the covenant, God's presence:

And it came to pass when the priests came out of the Most Holy Place (for all the priests who were present had sanctified themselves, without keeping to their divisions), and the Levites who were the singers, all those of Asaph and Heman and Jeduthun, with their sons and their brethren, stood at the east end of the altar, clothed in white linen, having cymbals, stringed instruments and harps, and with them one hundred and twenty priests sounding with trumpets indeed it came to pass, when the trumpeters and singers were as one, to make one sound to be heard in praising and thanking the Lord, and when they lifted up their voice with the trumpets and cymbals and instruments of music, and praised the Lord, saying: *"For He is good, For His mercy endures forever,"* that the house, the house of the Lord, was filled with a cloud, so that the priests could not continue ministering because of the cloud; for the glory of the Lord filled the house of God.

The entire nation of Israel gathered to dedicate the long-awaited temple of the Lord. Generations had waited for this magnificent structure, for they knew it was more than stubble and brick. This was the heart of their inheritance of the land, a place where God Himself would dwell as He promised. The tabernacle of David had already been in existence for thirty-three years, with twenty-four hour worship going on continuously. Yet this was the true temple, built under the reign of Solomon, containing the Most Holy Place into which they were now moving the ark of the covenant.

At such a historic moment, the Hebrew people knew that the sounding of their instruments was just as important as their prayers of thanksgiving. So on this day all the Levites stood at the east end of the altar, having already sanctified themselves. The chief musicians and their sons stood with the singers, percussionists, string players and one hundred and twenty Phil Driscolls blowing trumpets. Imagine that sound. Phil has been known to blow his trumpet and you can hear it as far as seven miles away. Can you imagine 120 of those guys lined up on the walls? Notice the priests of the Lord played silver trumpets, and they were dressed in white linen, which represented the purity of their lives. These were pure vessels of honor in the presence of God. They weren't just playing a tune, they were playing the very expression of their being. They understood music. They understood the fullness of this creative force that

God spoke into existence the very day He said, *"Let there be... "* (Genesis1:3). These were men who had feasted upon the Word of God their entire lives. They were full of the Word of God. When they began to play their instruments, they were not expecting hot licks. They expected the very light of God within their lives to flow out of their instruments, which were simply extensions of whom they were.

That's one of the reasons back then that a part of your job and daily work as a musician in the house of the Lord, was to build and construct your own instrument. David designed all of the instruments used in worship in the house of God, but each musician was required to build his own instrument. By the time he finished constructing it, he had a relationship with his instrument. He understood that his instrument was to be an expression and extension of who he was from the initial moment of its creation. The Bible says they all used the same kind of wood. After all the instruments to be played in the house of the Lord were made, the Bible says, that kind of wood was no longer found in the earth (I Kings 10:11-12). Boy, wouldn't you love to have an old D-28 Martin guitar made out of that stuff!

As stated in II Chronicles 5:13, "Indeed it came to pass, when the trumpeters and singers were as one, to make one sound to be heard in praising and thanking the Lord, and when they lifted up their voice with the trumpets and cymbals and instruments of music." When the blasting of prophetic declaration was perfectly combined in the spirit with the voice of man, the party started kicking! The phrase "were as one" literally speaks of one note, one sound in unison.

Notice they lifted up their "voice," not "voices." Revelation 19:6 says "And I heard, as it were, the voice of a great multitude, and as the sound of many waters and as the sound of mighty thunderings, saying 'Alleluia! For the Lord God Omnipotent reigns!'" This was one note, one purified, sanctified sound of Spirit-induced worship that came from the hearts and instruments of an entire nation.

When this sound pierced the heart of God, He responded with nothing less than His glory. It says the "priests could not continue ministering because of the cloud; for the glory of the Lord filled the house of God" (II Chronicles 5:14). Think of that. In the midst of joining His people with a truly holy sound, it's as if He knows we can't stand it any longer and fills the temple with Himself so we are forced to retreat. Don't we long to see the day when we all—preachers, platform teachers, musicians, and those who volunteer to clean the sanctuary after the service—are forced out of the temple because His presence is so strong? Are we willing to be that boldly interrupted?

When God's glory filled the temple, it was still not the end of the service for the Israelites. Solomon had the guts to stand up and speak in the midst of God's glory cloud. He declared before his people the goodness of his God. Solomon declared, *"The Lord said He would dwell in the dark cloud. But I have surely built You an exalted house, and a place for You to dwell in forever"* (II Chronicles 6:1-2). He reminded his people what the Lord promised through his father, David. Solomon's entire sermon and prayers display the transferral of what God deposited into David's heart moving into Solomon's heart of

65

wisdom. David literally shouted the praises of God into the next generation–into the very heart of his son, Solomon (see Psalms 145:4). As a result Solomon burned with desire to see a place of habitation for God among His people. The temple was finally built according to God's design.

It is imperative we understand that the temple was the place where God dwelt in the midst of His people. Imagine that, the very presence of God Himself. He chose to reveal Himself in the song or sound at the dedication or birthing of the temple. The significance of that event was fully realized at the birth of Jesus, the true ark, when God once again revealed Himself with a sound. His *Light* (sound) to the world exploded the heavens with a song that declared the name "Emmanuel–God with us" (see Matthew 1:23). A tike yet a temple, and the tearing down of that temple exploded again on the third day to fulfill the covenant and send His Spirit, His very

Presence to dwell in His people. Not with us but now in us–that we might be in one accord at the dedication of our lives as temples or dwelling places of God. Our unity in His presence welcomes the sound of heaven.

The Sound of Unity

The sound of heaven was heard in the temple during its dedication and during the night of King Jesus' birth. When was the next time we experienced this sound? In Acts 2, the disciples went to the upper room and did just as was done in the Old Testament.

In II Chronicles 5, they lifted up their voice *"as one"* with the trumpet. In Acts when the sound of heaven suddenly visits them again *"they were all with one accord in one place"* (Acts 2:1).

The sound came when that true unity—real unity—was there. The *real* unity. Unity for unity's sake isn't worth a flip. We keep trying to have unity meetings, but it's not going to happen. There's only one thing that will unite the body of Christ: When the center of the church is no longer the pulpit, but the center of the church is the throne of God. The definition of unity is corporate humility. That means none of us have any agendas, and none of us are trying to be responsible for just our little half-acre on the side of a mountain. God wants us to take the nations for Him, and we're just wanting to control our little half-acre!

Unity for unity's sake is just another form of religious humanism, because somewhere in the midst of that unity, people begin rallying around a person, an idea or a teaching. Though it might have started out of a pure heart, it becomes just another buzz. Gradually people begin desiring the anointing more than the presence of God. Then whoever is most anointed or whatever teaching is most powerful and moving becomes the thing that unites everyone. It's a seasonal thing. We're conditioned to believe there is power in numbers, and in some ways that's true. But there can only be fruit in numbers when God has the individuals' heart—individuals who are seeing and hearing what He's saying and doing, and uniting around that. God wants us to unite around His kingdom purposes rather than just kingdom exercises.

Kingdom exercises are the things we do, programs we establish and systems we build all in the name of furthering the kingdom. We turn our focus to those exercises so much that they become our little kingdoms. It becomes a noble thing to unite around secondary purposes because we present them in such a noble fashion. But if our unity is not solely around His throne, at best all those things can do is pacify us until He occupies us.

The disciples are in unity, and what happens? All of a sudden there is the sound as a mighty rushing wind coming through. I used to think, boy, all of sudden, this wind comes through, everybody's ears are pinned back, their hair's waving back and forth, there's quivering tongues of fire, shutters rattling around the sides of the upper room... what a scene! Boy, the Holy Ghost comes in style, doesn't He? But that's not at all what happened. The Bible says it was a sound *as* a rushing mighty wind. It was not a mighty rushing wind. This sound of heaven came rushing into that room and the church was born. The sound of heaven visited the earth the night Jesus was born and the night the church was born. As the sound of heaven becomes the sound of the earth, it won't just be an experience, but a birthing that takes place in the people of God.

There are prophetic connections between the sound visiting Solomon's temple, the upper room, and the continual worshiping assembly in heaven. The matching numbers aren't by coincidence. God's plan is always perfect, and when we slowly discover the intricacies involved in it, we're continually blown away. Notice the temple dedication. There were

24 choruses of musicians gathered, representing the 24 elders in Revelation worshiping before the throne of God, constantly falling on their face. At the temple dedication, there were also 120 trumpeters. There were 120 gathered in the upper room on the day of Pentecost. In Luke 24:50-53, we see that the group had returned to Jerusalem and were continually in the temple praising and worshiping God until the day He would send His promised Holy Spirit. Notice 500 people were initially invited, but only 120 showed up. Any time the Lord calls, He calls all. The majority reacts and the remnant responds. So the 120 were gathered in one accord, in one place—just like the assembly in II Chronicles—and suddenly there came a sound from heaven. The precursor was that they had to be in a *position* to hear the sound before they could actually hear it.

Does this now mean we have a formula for bringing the sound of many waters to earth? Sure, as much as we can move God with our flesh. The last person that tried that (or at least the most famous) was Uzza in I Chronicles 13:9. As I recall, he was fried on the highway in front of his friends and family. My point? There is nothing we can do to make God pour out the sounds of heaven on us but to obey Him. *"To obey is better than sacrifice"* (I Samuel 15:22). Through obedience we soon find ourselves sanctified as the priests on the day of dedication. Only now, on the other side of the cross, we are sanctified by the blood of Jesus and dressed in white robes not of ceremony but of radiant glory.

Every time the sound of many waters visits the earth, the entire generation is impacted by that release of God. I believe with my whole heart—and this is not just motivational writing or making a good point in a sermonette to "Christianettes"—that God wants to do something so dynamic that the entire next generation is going to experience it. *"The high praises of God"* are in our mouth and the *"two-edged sword"* is in our hand (see Psalm 149:6). The high praises take place when heaven touches earth and earth touches heaven. Then the execution of God's vengeance takes place (see Psalm 149: 6-9).

When the sound of heaven is magnified by the creative force of God releasing His authority to the Earth, the sound of corporate worship is heard. It is the sound of many waters and the sound of mighty thunder. In Revelation 14:2, John even heard these sounds of heaven combined with the *"sound of harpists playing their harps."* Every time that sound visited the Earth something phenomenal took place. When the sound that resonates out of the heart of God's people comes into agreement with the sound resonating out of God's heart, we find worship on earth as it is in heaven. To experience the worship of heaven is God's greatest desire for our lives.

Chapter Seven

Resistance and Sound

Heaven's sound of a rushing mighty wind is dependent on the element of resistance. Wind never makes a sound unless there is resistance. It can rush like rapids and be as mighty as the Grand Canyon and still remain silent. If you stand in the middle of a field on a beautiful sunny day and listen to the wind blowing by, it's not because it sings by itself. The wind makes a sound according to the resistance caused by your ears sticking out of your head, by the wheat stalks standing up from the ground or by the trees and leaves standing firm. Wind by itself is void of sound, but have it blow by something that is strongly rooted or grounded, and the music of wind is produced.

Man in his unredeemed state stands as a resistance to the wind of the Spirit. A man's spiritual state determines the sound coming out of his life. When you come into agreement with the sound of heaven, lining your life up with the heard order of God, your life takes on the anointing and blessing of all heaven. When you are in perpetual disagreement with God's sound, the sound coming out of your life will be more in tune with the enemy's plan to *"steal, kill and destroy"* you.

In a storm, wind doesn't make a sound until there's a resistance to rain. Though thunder resounds and shakes the earth while lightning lights up the sky, wind remains voiceless until combined with another element. It is the combination of rain and wind that creates the song. The same applies to a running brook. Water smashing steadily against firmly embedded rocks creates the sound of a river or stream.

Tubal-Cain, mentioned in Genesis 4:22 understood the powers of resistance and combining forces. He was the brother of Jubal, the father of music, and was skilled in working with iron. His craft involved striking an object against another, producing a clang reminiscent of early percussive instruments. Imagine Jubal observing his brother smite iron against iron, noticing how the sound got lower when Tubal-Cain used larger pieces and higher when smaller ones were involved. Imagine Jubal, the original musician with a mind bent toward spontaneous creativity, running off to create the first percussion instrument. Perhaps simple, curious observation of sounds produced from the resistance of one piece against another birthed an entire realm of sound incorporated into music. One definition of music is the manipulation of agreeing and disagreeing—or dissonant—tones.

The idea of resistance making music birthed a line of instruments. The Appalachian wind harp and Herrari harps are both created to play by themselves as a result of resistance. They are created in such a way that, hanging outside, the wind blows across the resistance of strings and causes them to vibrate, thus producing notes.

A harmonica is based on the same idea, as is a flute and all other woodwind and brass instruments. Resistance occurs when air is blown into an instrument. The instrument is created with chambers inside to provide a momentary "home" for the wind passing through. Notes are changed by increasing and decreasing the amount of time the breath experiences resistance inside the instrument. The amount of time changes with the lengthening or shortening of the internal chambers. That's why a tuba sounds different from a trumpet and a clarinet is different from an oboe.

Changing Sound

Imagine yourself standing out on a porch in the country. Your house is close to the railroad tracks, and like everyone else in your small town, life stops when a train comes through. Every conversation, every thought, every sound is immersed in the massive roar of a train passing through town. Often, during these moments of interruption, you take careful note of the sound you hear. You notice the sound changes as it nears. It starts faintly, with the periodic exclamation of the train's whistle being sounded. But as the train gets closer, you notice the pitch in your ear changing, becoming higher and louder. As the train passes in front of your house, you can hardly hear anything but the roar of the engine and the engineer blowing the ear-piercing scream of the train's whistle. You even feel the noise shaking the ground. Then as the train slowly slips into the distance, you again notice the amplitude changing. The noise becomes softer, its pitch lowering and returning to what it was when you could barely see the train approaching.

We can all relate to the relationship between sound and distance from experience with passing trains, cars, motorcycles or anything that moves past us with a sound. When the sound of heaven passes by, however, our hearing is changed. We look back on things differently. Though an approaching train is at a distance while you are standing on your porch, it has a particular note. When it passes by, the note changes volume. The moment of its greatest intensity is the same moment that the sound reaches a peak in its volume. And as it goes past you, it sounds like the note's pitch actually drops.

Compare this to a word from God in season. The word, like the sound of a train, does not change, though the bending of its pitch seems to indicate otherwise. Likewise, the Source of the sound does not change. What changes is the number of impulses reaching our ears per second. The impact the word or sound has upon our ears changes. So while the declaration and purposes of God in our lives stay the same, how we hear those words depends entirely upon where we stand. So let him who has an ear hear what the Spirit is saying to the church (see Revelation 2:7)

As in the train example, only our position relative to the source of sound changes. If Joe Country's house is a mile ahead of mine, he's hearing a different note being "played" by the train as it passes through town. Likewise, by the time it reaches his house, I'm hearing a lower pitch than he is. As the train goes by, its sound has less impact on my ear. As the Word of God "goes by" our lives through various seasons, we find the words having less impact on us than when they were relevant to our daily living.

All of this points to one thing: we need to be finely tuned and be ready to respond in season. The key to the train example is our position in hearing the sound. If the train's sound is going to maintain its pitch—if the sound is going to maintain its impact upon us—we must be on the train of heaven, not on the porch. If we're not part of the movement, we will spend our lives hearing the sound of heaven diminish as it goes by. It all has to do with our positional relationship to the sound, which is God's sound. It's as simple as that. If we want to be led by the sound of heaven as the Israelites were led by the cloud and pillar, then we must hop on board with the Source of the sound.

For example, currently the Lord is speaking loudly about bells, trumpets, and drums. For some reason He has chosen to sound these instruments as a wake-up call to his orchestra of warrior musicians. Now is the time to hear that sound and assimilate it to our hearts and lives. In music and sound, timing is everything, which brings the element of rhythm into music. How we respond to the music determines whether we will be in time or out of rhythm. It's a matter of hearing and responding.

Here is our hope: Christ is *in* us, *"the hope of glory"* (Colossians 1:27). If our lives in eternity were dependant upon our in-time response to God, we would all be as out of rhythm as a deaf man leading a marching band. The phrase *"Christ in you"* (Colossians 1:27) means to be hidden in Christ. It is not just a matter of the Master of the Universe being contained in us, but rather us contained in Him.

A Glorified Sound

Have you ever thought about why there's such a difference between a guitar and a trumpet? Or how about a trumpet and a cornet? What makes a trumpet sound like a trumpet and a cornet sound like a cornet? It all has to do with the vibrations reflecting off different pieces of matter in the instrument. The vibrations coming out of a trumpet are different from those coming out of a cornet. They have a different rate, frequency or even length. Therefore, a rounder, softer sound out of a trumpet and a higher, more direct sound from a cornet occurs. The sound produced from an instrument has everything to do with the size and texture of the material of the instrument from which it's reflecting. Every instrument ever made is unique, for it contains its own sound.

Sound through God's creation becomes individual and therefore, dependant upon the instrument. With our hope of glory–Christ dwelling in us–we produce a sound that's been in us since the beginning of time. We bring to life the full meaning of Emmanuel–Christ with us, Christ revealed in us. Isaiah 22:14 says, *"Then it was revealed in my hearing by the Lord of hosts."* Christ will be revealed as we hear His sound and release our individual, God-appointed sound as His unique instruments.

"Christ in you, the hope of glory" (Colossians 1:27). The word "glory" means "lightified." As stated earlier, light and sound are interchangeable, and made of the same properties. From this, we can say that Christ in you is the hope of being "lit," or the hope of being sounded. Christ is your hope of producing the sound that has resided in you since the beginning of time. Your sole purpose of existence as a worshiper of God is to be the personal instrument He created you to be, and played for His glory. Within the very truth of the living Christ is the assurance that you will be played before God.

Resolved Tension

What is seen in the spirit can be seen in the natural. So it is with the spiritual make-up of music. There are three notes that make up a chord–first, third and fifth. There are three parts that make up God–Father, Son, and Holy Spirit. Likewise, as we are made in the image of God, there are three parts that make up man–spirit, soul, and body. Anyone who knows anything about playing the piano knows the fingering to a major chord involves the thumb, middle finger, and pinky. When you drop the middle finger one note, you have a minor chord, which creates a tension in the music. When you play a fourth note–your fourth finger–in place of the third, creates what is called a suspended chord. At its base level, music is made up of tension and release. When the middle note of a chord is dropped or replaced by something else (like a suspended chord), it creates a tension that can only be resolved by again playing the first, third and fifth notes of a major chord.

In the spirit realm when you drop the Son, you end up with a minor chord. For centuries denominations and people groups have dropped part of the Holy Triad. Many embraced the Father and cast down the deity of His Son. Others who have accepted the deity of the Son have forsaken the Holy Spirit. The result is, and always has been, tension. There can be no resolve until the right notes are played—until the three intended parts are accepted as part of the whole chord. If there's no relationship with the Son, there can be no revealing of the Father. If there's no relationship with the Holy Spirit, there can be no revelation of the Son, who points us to the Father.

This brings us back to the meaning of Emmanuel, Christ revealed in or to us. The word "reveal" literally means "to strip or denude, to show, to make known, to tell or to uncover." As Christ is revealed to us, we are revealed to the Holy Spirit and drawn by Him back to our original union with the Father. We have to understand we are not just bodies that happen to have a spirit included as part of the package. We are spirits who just happen to have a body. Too often we rely on everything but the Holy Spirit in our spirit man for our senses. Again, we are made up of three parts: spirit, soul, and body. Our body is always environmentally conscious. Our soul is always self-conscious, and our spirit is God-conscious. Our mistake is that we deal with the things of the Spirit by the soul, which robs us of our spirit of revelation.

I Corinthians 2:9-10 says, "Eye has not seen, nor ear heard, Nor have entered into the heart of man The things which God has prepared for those who love Him. But God has revealed them to us through His Spirit. For the Spirit searches all things, yes, the deep things of God." As we talk about the sound of heaven, it's essential to understand that our eyes have *not* seen and our ears have *not* heard. Our soulish senses cannot take in the truth of God. But it is His Spirit within us, Emmanuel—that reveals. As we hop on board the train rather than just let it pass us by, we become hidden in Him and He is revealed in us. The sound we previously heard from afar suddenly becomes the same sound He is playing through our lives.

Chapter Eight

Ringing the Bells of Heaven

There's little doubt that some of the earliest musical instruments created were percussion instruments. The Bible names Jubal as being the *"father of all those who play the harp and flute"* (Genesis 4:21). This passage in Genesis 4 only mentions the harp and the flute or pipe, which were instruments of strings and wind. Yet some historical accounts report that Jubal caught the first suggestion of his art from the ring of his brother Tubal-Cain's hammer on his anvil. Early musical notes sounded by a blow on some tone-producing object such as wood or a rock most likely produced tones that were not definite and clear. However, we do know they were a result of percussion.

In Genesis 31:27 Laban says to Jacob, *"I might have sent you away with joy and songs, with timbrel and harp."* This was the second mention of music in the Bible. Here we see the music of strings mingled with the sounds produced by striking the tightened skin of the timbrel. The song of praise through which Miriam and her maidens celebrated the triumphant exodus from Egypt was accompanied exclusively by timbrels. These instruments resembled the modern-day tambourine, in which a drum-like sound produced by tapping upon the skin is mingled with the jingling of small metal plates striking together, as the timbrel is swung or shaken in the air.

Musical instruments evolved out of the very early age of civilization. Interesting illustrations are found in the musical history of the Asian nations. They have retained their musical history through many ages. One of the most elaborate instruments known to the Chinese is the *king*, invented by one of their emperors more than two thousand years before Christ. It consists of sixteen flat stones suspended in two ranks within a frame. The stones were of different sizes and shapes, so that when it was struck with a wooden mallet it produced a varied scale of notes. They also used drums of every kind and size, rows of copper plates, clappers of wood, and wooden tubs struck with a hammer and huge cymbals. A picture of a Japanese native orchestra that was engraved in Siebold's work on Japan shows seven performers playing a flute, a large drum shaped like an hourglass, two small drums, two bell rattles and a set of wooden clappers. In this engraving, out of the seven instruments, all but one is a percussion instrument. Other Asian nations exhibit similar instrumentation, although wind and string instruments play a larger role in many. This primitive yet widespread discovery of tones being produced by blows or strikes on stones and metal brings understanding of the beginnings of the bell.

In early art, pictures resemble the modern bell in its shape. There should be no surprise to find many early authors of poetry and literature making numerous allusions to the use of bells as a musical instrument. The book of Exodus gives us the earliest mention of bells in Scripture. It speaks of small golden bells which tinkled around the hem of the Levitical high priest (see Exodus 28:33). Also, Zechariah spoke of the bells adorning the harnesses of the horses (see Zechariah 14:20).

The striking of bells is a sound that has been heard in the ears of man almost from his beginning. I challenge you to try and buy a new synthesized keyboard that does not include bell-oriented sounds. Even today, though the sounds are synthesized or synthetic—and from keyboard to keyboard there will be noticeable changes in the tones and resonance of the bells. It's obvious! Bells have a sound that still incites an emotional response from listeners today. Suffice it to say, bells to one degree or another have impacted every generation since the beginning of music. Throughout history, if there has been an impact in the natural, I can assure you there has been an impact in the spirit realm. The bell is an instrument of proclamation.

Calling Them In

The role of a messenger boy, page, or town herald has long been replaced with television, radio, and endless other means of electronic communication. What used to be announced with human voice has turned into words on a computer screen or a catchy jingle on a television commercial. Did you ever wonder why we call them jingles?

Few things grab the ear as quickly as the ringing of a bell. For centuries, people have used the sound of metal clanging against metal to grab the attention of hearts everywhere. There is more to this gripping sound, however.

The bell has always been a means to call people in. Such spiritual heroes as Charles Wesley and George Whitfield used bells to call people into the middle of their towns so they could preach to them. Bells have been used inside the belfries of the world's grandest cathedrals, where it has often required up to sixty men to ring them. Bells were rung in the tiny steeples of the smallest country churches, where a smiling old deacon would call in the worshipers. Wherever they were rung, they were rung with one intent—to draw those from miles away into the house of God.

The bell has also been forever connected with preachers and prophets, those declaring and bringing forth the word of the Lord. John Knox and George Fox walked through the middle of their cities ringing bells while declaring the word of the Lord over the land. These men believed in the reality of releasing what was in the spirit with a natural sound. Unfortunately this belief was twisted into sheer superstition. During the same era it was believed a bell was to be rung whenever a person died. As soon as the dying breathed their last breath, a witness would ring the bell in hopes of startling the evil spirits waiting to capture the person's soul. They believed this gave the person a head start in finding their way into eternity without the evil spirits getting them first. Though superstitious, it's important to note how these people were still aware of the spiritual release behind the sounding of a bell.

The bells in Europe had yet another purpose. Before the invention of the watch, bells were the primary keepers of time. Throughout the day, townspeople were able to mark the time by the bells which started at 6:00 a.m. and rang every three hours. The one exception to this three-hour system was the curfew bell which rang at 8:00 p.m. This was the notification of sleeping time, or translated from French, the "time to cover the fires." In fact the French word for curfew is *couvre-feu*, to "cover the fire." Following a night of rest, the bells would resume again at 6:00 a.m. and the fires would be started again.

The bells of the Holy Spirit are being rung now to awaken a sleeping church. Musician Keith Green once phrased us as a people "asleep in the Light." The fires of our self-induced, self-maintained revivals are being covered by the hand of God, and we are seeing His revival fires lit sporadically across the world. These are the fires of truth, and the bells heard are the sounds of this truth.

Bells not only announce and declare but also pronounce imminent war. In the eleventh and twelfth century, most war ships had bells mounted to them. While a lookout was in the crow's nest, the sound of wind and water was so loud that it was impossible for others to hear his shouts warning of approaching enemies. To make sure everyone on board heard the warning cry, he used the bell to alert the crew of nearing ships. This ringing was a call to war. Upon hearing it, every crew member prepared himself for battle. Many today have heard the call to war in their spirit. God is now sending the sound to declare the call. The time for war is being marked with the very bells of heaven.

We must take the sound we hear to heart. Bells have always been the forerunning sound of revival. They have been used for the calling of warriors, for the marking of time and the calling of service (thus we have the term "bell captain"). They have been used ceremoniously for blessings and curses throughout generations since the book of Leviticus. During times of war, they have been stolen from abbey towers and melted down to make weapons and instruments of war. For instance, in Richmond, Virginia, the Second Baptist Church donated their bronze bells to Robert E. Lee's Confederate army to be melted down and made into cannons. And during times of peace, these cannons and other weapons of war have been in turn melted down and made back into bells. In peace or war we cannot lose sight of the meaning and purpose of bells. We must heed the sound that so pierces our spirits.

Christmas Bells

Nothing is as beautiful as the sound of bells that ring across the nations of the world at Christmas time. It is a tradition that began to mark one of the chief festivals and fasts of the Christian year. The tradition differed at times from country to country, but England was responsible for the prominence of the event. At one time in history, England was called the "ringing island." Bells were used to follow the course of the church's year in marking the various seasons, festivals, and fasts. As the year neared its end, it was common to hear bells ringing from the steeple of the local parish church once or twice a week. Of all the times the bells were rung during the year, the ringing of the joyous bells of Christmas was undoubtedly the most glorious event of the year.

The ringing of the devil's knell on Christmas Eve was one of the most curious and noteworthy uses of bells during the Christmas season. It is alleged that the bells were rung in celebration of the night Christ was born, when He eternally destroyed and broke the power of the evil one over man. The bells would ring from midnight until two o'clock in the morning. All the bells of England would be rung simultaneously, proclaiming joy and liberty to all mankind. Wouldn't you have loved to have been sitting on a cloud and heard the blending of bells ranging from 432,000 pounds down to two ounces and all proclaiming, "GLORY TO GOD IN THE HIGHEST" (Luke 2:14).

For years we've heard prophets declare the coming of a new sound. From the thundering roar of earthquakes to the slightest rush of wind, God is speaking. In His faithfulness, the Holy Spirit is quickening the people of God to be sensitive to sound. Whether it is heard from a 432,000-pound bell or a two-ounce bell, *"He that has an ear, let him hear what the Spirit says to the churches"* (Revelation 2:7).

Chapter Nine

Trumpets, Shofars and Ram's Horns

Whenever the sounding of a trumpet is mentioned in Scripture, a significant event follows. From its first mention in Exodus 19:13, establishing the law of God, to the seven blasts in Revelation 8:6 and Revelation 1o, which still resound today, the blowing of the trumpet marks the very announcement of God's presence. Imagine the day all of God's people were gathered at the foot of Mount Sinai.

In Exodus 19:16-19, the scene is set:

Then it came to pass on the third day, in the morning, that there were thunderings and lightnings, and a thick cloud on the mountain; and the sound of the trumpet was very loud, so that all the people who were in the camp trembled. And Moses brought the people out of the camp to meet with God, and they stood at the foot of the mountain. Now Mount Sinai was completely in smoke, because the Lord descended upon it in fire. Its smoke ascended like the smoke of a furnace, and the whole mountain quaked greatly. And when the blast of the trumpet sounded long and became louder and louder, Moses spoke, and God answered him by voice.

The audible voice of God was connected to the sound of the trumpet, along with thunder, lightning, fire, and smoke. In Exodus 20:18: "Now all the people witnessed the thunderings, the lightning flashes, the sound of the trumpet, and the mountain smoking; and when the people saw it, they trembled and stood afar off."

God spoke and His voice was thunder, lightning, smoke, and the sounding of a loud trumpet. He basically grabbed the desert and mountain and shook them. Immediately after, we find God's people saying, "Moses, go and tell God that He will be our God, we will be His people. We'll go where He tells us to go, we'll do what He tells us to do, we'll walk in obedience to His will, if He just won't speak to us anymore." How often do we find ourselves in this same situation? "God, I'll do anything You want me to do, I'll go anywhere You want me to go. I'll be anything You want me to be, if You'll just speak to me!" Then when God begins to speak, He shakes everything in our lives. Thunder and lightning begin to rage, and storms begin to blow. The fire of God begins to devour things in our lives. And suddenly we say, "God, I will teach Sunday school. I'll be a deacon. I'll be a good testimony. I'll be anything . . . but just don't speak to me anymore!" We begin to close ourselves off from the voice of God and choose the comforts of religious Christianity instead. I submit to you that the voice of the Lord is about to be heard so distinctly that lines will be drawn and wars will be fought the likes of which we have never seen. We must be a people willing to hear the sound of the trumpet without shrinking back, but pursuing the mountain of the Lord's presence. Without a doubt there is a prophetic trumpet being sounded today that will be accompanied by the thunder of heaven and the lightning of God's presence. It will devour everything in our lives that might cause us to shrink back because of its awesome nature and power.

Throughout Scripture, the awesome trumpet sound could be heard to call soldiers to war, pronounce death to an enemy, mark the days of atonement, declare times of jubilee, tear down the walls of Jericho, or call the people of God to worship. There has always been a significant spiritual force behind the resonance in a trumpet's call.

In Revelation 1:10, we find one of the many times the source of this spiritual force is revealed. John writes, *"I was in the Spirit on the Lord's Day, and I heard behind me a loud voice, as of a trumpet."* In Revelation 4:1, he says, *"The first voice which I heard was like a trumpet speaking with me, saying, 'Come up here, and I will show you things which must take place after this.'"* The voice of God is repeatedly described as sounding like a trumpet. As the Lord identifies Himself in Revelation, He declares to John the revelation of Jesus with His voice as the sound of a trumpet. To grasp the revelation, He beckons John to *"come up here."* With God's voice—the blaring of a trumpet—we are called into a higher place of revelation and worship of Jesus Christ.

The voice John *heard* quickly becomes *vision.* Immediately after hearing the loud voice in the beginning of the first chapter, he turns towards the voice and sees seven lamp stands (see Revelation 1:12). From this point on, his vision increases and the sights and sounds of the heavens are opened up to him. The Lord's voice (or in John's case, the voice of the angel) came as a trumpet and as *"the sound of rushing waters"* (see Revelation 1:15). He speaks through both with the same power and significance.

The Blast on High Street

While traveling throughout the British Isles in 1998, the group I was with had many unique encounters. As I write this, the memory of an event in Edinburgh, Scotland, keeps cropping up in my spirit. Though at the time it seemed small, I am continually realizing its significance and timeliness to what God is saying.

As typical tourists, the members of our group had split up that afternoon to scour the streets of Edinburgh for souvenirs and traditional Scottish items. We had just visited the city's main castle, where we were able to see the Stone of Destiny, the Scottish war memorial and the historical fortresses and cannons of protection upon the city's summit. After this we walked down High Street from the castle to the home of John Knox, where we tasted of the godliness and devotion of Scotland's great evangelist and prophet. Upon stepping out of his home, the contrast of the peacefulness of Knox's home to the crowded streets was powerful. High Street was a sightseeing mecca lined with tourist shops, New Age shops, restaurants and cafes, a cathedral, and endless other attractions to entice visitors.

As one of the thousands walking this street, I wandered into a souvenir shop. A couple from Texas was also with us on the trip. While glancing over the rows of decorations and souvenirs, my friend found a huge cow horn with a trumpet mouthpiece attached to it, which he immediately recognized as a "Texas shofar." He asked the shop-owner if he could step outside and try it out, to which he was given permission. Little did the shop-owner know that God had spoken to the Texan to sound the blast of a trumpet on High Street.

In the midst of the passing buses, taxis, and cars, with thousands of people milling through the streets, suddenly—without warning—a powerful blast of sound reflected off the surrounding buildings and cobblestone sidewalks at a mind-boggling volume. The blast was heard from Edinburgh castle to John Knox's home—almost eight blocks. Though I couldn't see where it came from, I immediately knew who was responsible for this explosion of sound. I was paying for a postcard at the store counter of a bustling shop when the sound hit. I noticed the reactions of people around me. Every person in the shop froze in their tracks. The look on people's faces was as if to say, "What was that? Where did that come from? What should we do?" Everyone in the store was stunned to silence. Just as everyone quietly resumed their movements, the sound came again.

91

This time people scurried towards the windows to determine what was going on. It was as if a storm warning or some emergency had taken place. The lady behind the counter asked, "What is it?" to which I jokingly replied, "I bet you a dollar to a doughnut there's a big Texan on the other end of this deal."

I made my way to the door, past the people peering out the window, when the third blast came. As I walked past a Scottish gentleman, he said, "My God, that's remarkable!" I stepped out onto the sidewalk and looked across the street. There my friend stood with a huge grin on his face as he saw the stunned look on the faces of people. The street had virtually come to a halt. After a few moments, things returned to normal and the clutter of street sound resumed its dominance in the air.

What most caught my attention about the scene was the response of the people. Upon hearing the first blow, virtually every person on the street was stilled. From this abrupt halt of regular momentum there was a sense of wonder, from the simple "What is that?" to the more introspective, "What should I do?" The initial sounding of God often leaves people stunned, walking around as if in a daze. The second sounding drew people in. Shoppers ignored their search for items, to instead find the source behind the sound. Their attention was fully on figuring out what this was all about. By the third blast of the trumpet, people were amazed. The man remarking, "My, that's remarkable," typified our natural amazement with sound. Yet following this, he and the rest of the streetwalkers simply resumed their activities.

Their apathetic reaction astonished me. In I Corinthians 14:8 (NIV), Paul writes, *"If the trumpet does not sound a clear call, who will get ready for battle?"* My friend's trumpet call was clear—clear enough for a stretch of eight blocks to stop its motion. Yet how clear are our spiritual ears when we can hear such a blast in the spirit realm and respond by momentarily wondering, only to eventually resume our own activity? Is this a simple case of "He who has an ear let him hear?" I believe it's more than that. As end-time people, we are in the midst of hearing a trumpet sound with undeniable clarity. The Lord is sounding His trumpet to the nations. Many are saying, "What is it?" only to go right back to what they're doing. However, we know from the seven angels sounding their trumpets in Revelation 8 that the final trumpet calls will be heard by everyone and will bring judgment and destruction. In the midst of those calls is heard, *"Woe! Woe! Woe to the inhabitants of the earth, because of the trumpet blasts about to be sounded by the other three angels!"* (Revelation 8:13 NIV).

These trumpet calls are not playful melodies to slowly awaken us from our slumber; they are powerful and destructive blasts that split the ear and separate the saved from the unsaved. They are declarations of the righteousness and holiness of God. For years, prophets and evangelists have sounded their trumpets to bring people back into the house of God. We must now pray for the anointing to be one of those called to sound the trumpet. Pray that their blast will cause the army of the Lord to truly prepare for the battle at hand. Even more, we must pray for a clear sound to be released, one which is heard undeniably by every living creature and causes us to respond with immediate, Spirit-induced change.

Shofars and Silver Trumpets

There are two types of trumpets used in the Bible. The shofar is depicted more than eighty times as being either a ram's horn or a trumpet. In traditional Israel, however, it was called a ram's horn. As I stated earlier, it is first mentioned in Exodus 19:16, where the voice of the trumpet was heard in relation to the voice of the Lord. In Exodus 19:18, according to the Torah, the sound was so penetrating, the people could actually *see* the sound. But that is not the first mention of the ram's horn. The ram's horn, first mentioned in Exodus 19:13, is a reminder of Abraham's sacrifice of Isaac and God's provision of a ram as a substitute. The shofar was blown at the start of the jubilee year of *Yom Kippur* in Leviticus 25:9. Does this make you wonder where Jubal got his name? The father of music's name, Jubal, literally means "trumpet." The trumpet was used to announce the beginning of the festivals in Numbers 10:2. In Joshua 6, the battle of Jericho was won with the blast of the trumpet. Gideon and his army used the sound of the trumpet for a victory in Judges 7. The Israelites used the shofar to signal the assembly during war times in Judges 3, II Samuel 20 and Amos 3. It was also used for the coronation of kings. King Solomon was an example of this in I Kings 1. In Psalm 47 the shofar reminded Israel that God is sovereign. During temple ceremonies in Jerusalem, the shofar was used

to accompany other musical instruments during times
of celebration, as in Psalm 98. According to Isaiah 27
the shofar will be used at the end, gathering the exiles
to Israel. The blowing of the shofar is a call to
repentance in Isaiah 58 and a warning in Ezekiel 33
and Numbers 10. The shofar ushers in the day of the
Lord in Joel 2.

In the New Testament, the shofar is sounded at
the resurrection of the dead in I Thessalonians 4:16.
John was taken up to heaven in Revelation 4 by the
sound of the shofar, where we find seven trumpets as
God judges the earth during tribulation. There are
many more references to the trumpet, the shofar and
the ram's horn. These are just a few to give you an
idea of the significance of this instrument that creates
such a powerful sound.

The second kind of trumpet in the Bible is the
silver trumpet. Numbers 10:1-10 gives us information
about the silver trumpets:

*And the Lord spoke to Moses, saying: "Make
two silver trumpets for yourself; you shall make
them of hammered work; you shall use them for
calling the assembly and for directing the movement
of the camps. "When they blow both of them, all the
congregation shall gather before you at the door of
the tabernacle of meeting. "But if they blow only one,
then the leaders, the heads of the divisions of Israel,
shall gather to you. "When you sound the advance,
the camps that lie on the east side shall then begin
their journey. "When you sound the advance the
second time, then the camps that lie on the south side*

shall begin their journey; they shall sound the call for them to begin their journeys. "And when the assembly is to be gathered together, you shall blow, but not sound the advance. "The sons of Aaron, the priests, shall blow the trumpets; and these shall be to you as an ordinance forever throughout your generations. "When you go to war in your land against the enemy who oppresses you, then you shall sound an alarm with the trumpets, and you will be remembered before the Lord your God and you will be saved from your enemies. "Also in the day of your gladness, in your appointed feasts, and at the beginning of your months, you shall blow the trumpets over your burnt offerings and over the sacrifices of your peace offerings; and they shall be a memorial for you before your God: I am the Lord your God.

First, notice there were two different trumpets: a trumpet of assemblage and a trumpet of alarm. At the sound of one trumpet, all the people assembled themselves as a congregation, but at the blowing of an alarm, they would advance and go forward. Notice it also says when the priests were to blow these trumpets, *"These shall be to you as an ordinance forever throughout your generations"* (verse 8). When they went to war against their enemies, they were to blow an alarm with the trumpets. God would hear the sound, remember them, and save them. It was more than just a tradition. There was a continual remembrance of the promises of God and His power to fulfill His covenant. The trumpet sound caused the hearts of men to tremble at the greatness of the God of Israel. At the sound, they knew they must assemble or reject the instructions of their God. Notice that His instructions were prompted by the sounding of the trumpet.

The trumpet was also blown for days of gladness, solemn days, and the beginning of months. They were blown over their burnt offerings and peace offerings for the purpose of being a memorial or reminder that God was indeed their God. On each Sabbath in the temple, two men with silver trumpets and a man with a shofar would make three trumpet blasts twice during the day. They would bring forth a staccato sound with the horn, which is the word *teruah*, meaning "shout." A sign of dedication on the temple wall said, "To the house of the blowing of the trumpet."

Rosh Hashanah is the day of the blowing of the trumpets. The original name was *Yom Teruah. Yom* means "day" and *teruah* means "shout." From this we have the staccato sound, or the shout, of the horn. According to the *Mishnah,* the trumpet used for *Rosh Hashanah* is the ram's horn, rather than those made of metal or silver. A shofar, or ram's horn, delivers the first blast, a silver trumpet the second, and then the shofar sounded again for the third. When our English Bible use the word trumpet, most of the time they refer to the ram's horn. Today in Israel, because there is no temple, the silver trumpet is not used, and in its place the kudu shofar is used. The large shofars seen today in many praise and worship gatherings and conferences are more accurately called Yemenite shofars. These larger Yemenite shofars come from the kudu, which is an African antelope. It is used in many congregations as a call to worship.

Throughout Scripture, trumpets from many sizes, shapes, pitches, and tones have been used to demonstrate different acts, workings and memorials to God. The trumpet is used in countless ways of worship, but by and large, it is an instrument of the prophetic. The words trumpet, silver trumpet, shofar and ram's horn have become conversationally interchangeable—and to a degree, rightfully so. The first mention of horns in the Bible is one of the most prophetically significant happenings in all of Scripture.

As stated in Genesis 22:13-14, Then Abraham lifted his eyes and looked, and there behind him was a ram caught in a thicket by its horns. So Abraham went and took the ram, and offered it up for a burnt offering instead of his son. And Abraham called the name of the place, Jehovah-Jirah; as it is said to this day, In the Mount of the Lord it shall be provided. It is undetermined at what point in history the horns could be taken from a ram's head, hollowed out, and release a blast of air creating a tone. But the prophetic reality is that a ram lost his life and was sacrificed on behalf of Abraham, Isaac, Jacob and the many generations to come. The horns of a ram had become a trumpet by the time Moses and the children of Israel met God at the foot of Mount Sinai. The trumpets sounded loud and long as God demonstrated his power to keep His covenant with the people. Leviticus 25:9 says, "Then you shall cause the trumpet of the Jubilee to sound on the tenth day of the seventh month; on the Day of Atonement you shall make the trumpet to sound throughout all your land." This was the continuation of God's covenant being declared with the trumpet on the Day of Atonement. Throughout Scripture, the festivals, feasts, and fasts were accompanied by trumpets, used as both calls to worship and as declarations commemorating the acts of God toward the children of Israel.

Jesus was the Lamb sacrificed to finally bring that covenant to its fulfillment. It's interesting to note the reference to the horn in the story of His birth in Luke 16:9. *"Blessed is the Lord God of Israel, for He has visited and redeemed His people, and has raised up a horn of salvation for us in the house of His servant David."* From Genesis to Revelation the sound of the trumpet has always played a part in redeeming and reminding us of God's eternal position. From the ram to the lamb, the trumpet is still sounding today for every man in his unredeemed state. Those who have embraced this reality have become new creations, accepting the fulfillment of the covenant. We are commanded in Scripture to praise God for the awesome things He has done.

Lightning, thunder, and a cloud of smoke vibrated heaven and earth around Mount Sinai, and the first trumpet was heard in all of its awesome power. If the first sound of the trumpet was that awesome, what will the last trumpet sound like? The last trumpet in Scripture will be the blast of Gabriel's horn, calling forth the hosts of earth to join the hosts of heaven in a praise that will never end. I can't biblically validate what I am about to say, but I wouldn't be a bit surprised if Gabriel has not already taken his trumpet out from its case, placed it to his lips and inhaled.

Chapter Ten

Drums of Thunder

Since its creation, the drum has always been an instrument of thunder. During the years of the Triangular Slave Trade, African tribes used drums to pray for rainstorms of protection to ward off slave traders. The war drums of the Scottish Highlands were used to strike fear into their enemies with their thunderous sound. Even in the United States, our revolutionary and civil wars were fought to the beat of drums resounding through the hills and mountains. In fact, you can find the use of drums in every war and army throughout history. What element does this instrument possess that it has always been the marker of war? Furthermore, what mysterious quality has made it a controversial subject in modern Christianity? What is it about rhythm that enflames the spirit of religion to create such a breeding ground for "beat-a-phobics?"

I use the word "beat-a-phobics" in order to offend you early if you cater to the belief that drums are of the devil. I recently spoke at a seminar and was responding to questions in regards to music. The statement was made that there are no drums to be found in any concordance or Scripture. My reply was,

"Sure, they're in there—right under the verse on pianos, next to the passage on restrooms and Sunday school. There are many things in Scripture not spelled out with our modern-day understanding. The great, great, great-grandfather of the drums is found throughout Scripture, just as you can find the great, great, great-grandfather of the piano and the great, great, great-grandfather of Sunday school and restrooms." Remember the dung gate? (Just kidding). Then I collected myself, repented for my sarcasm and went ahead, which is what I intend to do now.

It is a biblical reality that drums were used in Scripture to offend the enemies of God. If you are offended by rhythm or by a particular beat and have bought the idea that a particular beat can conjure up demonic spirits and release them in the church, I hope the truth you're about to hear doesn't just offend you. I hope it's a truth that sets you free.

The fact is, rhythm was created by God, not the devil. A song with a beat is not the enemy of piety. According to *Webster,* rhythm is a "regularity or flow of movement which groups by recurrent heavy and light accents or beats." Let me say again, the devil did not create rhythm. God created rhythm. If your heart gets out of rhythm, you'll understand very quickly that God created rhythm for His purposes. You can stand on the seashore and the ocean's waves will crash against the rocks in perfect rhythm, for God created them to do so. Let's see how *Webster* defines the word beat. Bear in mind, I use a *Webster's* dictionary written in the 1800s, before the humanists influenced it. Mentally apply these definitions and thoughts as to be used against the enemy, not against the purposes of God. "Beat" means "to strike repeatedly; to lay on repeated blows with a stick or with the hand, or with any instrument; to render punishment; to strike an instrument of music; to play on, as a drum; to break, bruise or pulverize by beating or pounding; to strike; to tread, as a path (a beaten path); to overcome in battle, contest or strife; to vanquish or conquer, as one beats another; to beat down; to break, destroy or throw down by beating or battering; to press down or lay flat, as by treading, by a current of water or by a violent wind; to depress or crush; a recurring stroke; a pulsation, as a beat of the pulse." Get the idea?

Webster defines the word "drum" as "a marshal instrument of music, in the form of a hollow cylinder and covered at the ends with a skin or hide; the drum of the ear, to the tympanum or barrel of the ear—the membrane which receives the vibrations of air and sound." Now let's look to the time of the great, great, great-grandfathers of instruments, before pianos had keys, trumpets had valves, guitars had amplifiers, and dung gates had porcelain bowls.

Timbrels and Cymbals

Before the drums evolved into today's elaborate sets of multi-sized kits, the instruments and the mechanics of playing the instruments were quite different. Modern drums were born out of what we consider to be the early biblical percussion instruments such as tabrets, timbrels, tambourines and bells. Each of these required a striking action producing a percussive tone, which in turn produced the striking or beating of sound on the ear drum. In its truest definition, a piano is a percussion instrument because the tone is produced by the striking of hammers or small mallets upon metal strings. The xylophone and marimba are percussion instruments that pre-date what we know to be the piano. There are many variations of these instruments, such as the clavichord, harpsichord and even the hammer dulcimer. All these instruments were first used as a result of striking two objects together, which produced sounds and eventually evolved into instruments that would produce tones. In Exodus 28:33-34, we see that on the hem of the priest's garment there were pomegranates and bells of gold. The Hebrew word "bells" is the word *pah-gamohn*, which simply means "as struck." It's translated "bell" only twice in Scripture. Today we do not find a wide use of bells as musical instruments in Judaic culture. However, they did exist, and a variation of the bell was the cymbal, which we will look at in a moment. The principle of the striking of bells that we have already covered obviously gave them their name. It's also obvious the bell was a model of a larger instrument that was evidently struck. Thus, we have the clapper or striker inside the bell or the mallet used to strike the outside.

Cymbals, like bells, were instruments that would sound through vibration. The Hebrew word for cymbal is *tz'lah-tzahl*. It employs the idea of vibration—to tinkle or to rattle together. "Cymbal" means "to clatter, as in clanging together," and is used in II Samuel 6:5 and Psalm 150:5. The Hebrew word *m'tzil-tah-yim* tells us that the cymbals are doubled. This word is used in I Chronicles 13:8; 15:16, 19, 28;

16:5, 42; Ezra 3:10 and Nehemiah 12:27. Strangely enough, this word is also translated "bells" in Zechariah 14:20. To put this in proper context, one referred to the clattering of a cymbal, while the other dealt with numerous cymbals rattling against each other in the same fashion as the small two-inch cymbals on the side of a tambourine. This reminds us of what drummers today call high-hats or trap-cymbals. The Greek word *kumbalon* is a cymbal spoken of in I Corinthians 13:1 as a hollow cymbal. There are two main types of cymbals used: the loud cymbals and the high-sounding cymbals, both seen in Psalm 150. When we look at II Samuel 6:5, we see the word cornets. This word is wrongly translated. It's the word *m'nah-gan-geem*, and means a "sistrum," called so because of its rattling sound. It's an instrument with metal rods on metal rings that move up and down when shaken back and forth. These cymbals were typically made of brass. I Corinthians 13:1 referred to these cymbals as the sounding of brass. When David rode back into the city after the slaughter of the Philistines, the women of Israel met him with three-stringed instruments which kept rhythm while they sang prophetically and danced. We know it was a prophetic song because the lyrics were, *"Saul has slain his thousands, but David his ten thousands"* (I Samuel 29:5). David had not slain his ten thousands yet. It was the beginning of his career. The instrument they used was the *shah-leesh*. It was a musical instrument in the form of a triangle with small stones and cymbals that created a rattling, jingling sound.

Many times in Scripture we see the word "timbrel." In Exodus 15:20, Psalm 81:2 and 150:4, this word literally means "to drum." The word *tohph* is often translated "timbrel," and on other occasions as "tabret." As time progressed, these grandfathers of the modern-day drums continued to evolve. Eventually these instruments, used to establish the cadence and rhythm of poetry and prophecy, grew into drums as large as a truck. In the ancient writings and art from every nation, the use of percussion instruments and drums is mentioned. Pagan nations such as Egypt and Assyria used drums as well. To this day, drums are used with an anointing of an unholy spirit in idolatry. Although sometimes there is a perversion of rhythms, gestures, and releases of emotion that employ drums, I dare say God never intended for us to throw away what He designed to be used in our worship of Him. We are to be a people of redemption and restoration, anointed of the Holy Spirit, to exercise *all* of our creativity and demonstrate *all* of our emotions as we submit our spirits, souls, and bodies to show forth the praises of God. Drums were used to augment and enhance the dynamics and expressions of worship, and must continue to serve that purpose today.

In Rhythm with God

Like you, I have heard the argument that African jungle music has the power to conjure up evil and stir our minds and emotions to lust, cannibalize, and take part in every other ungodly expression. I've heard it said that those things are brought about as a result of evil music. But I declare to you music is not moral or immoral. It's amoral. Music is nothing more than an outward expression of the inward health or sickness of our spirits. God created music. God also created all the components of music and deposited within every man, woman, and child a desire to worship. Remember music is not worship. Music is a means God has given us to express worship. If we are not worshipers of God with our music, we have forfeited the reason we exist, for He created us as worshipers. There are people all over the world who resist the music of the church because it's not aggressive enough. It doesn't have that driving edge they relate to in music. There are also people in the church all over the world that resist the aggressive sounds because they feel God would be displeased with such extreme, aggressive expression.

Many in the church today can remember the emotional hoops they jumped through just to come to a place where they could actually raise their hands in a public demonstration of praise. For some, clapping hands to the beat of a song in church seemed like blasphemy. The fact of the matter is God desires for us to sing, dance, clap our hands, be clamorously foolish, and like David, praise Him with all our might.

Every one of the seven words translated "praise" in Scripture requires a bodily function. When we see the word "praise" it is a prompting to sing, clap, kneel, shout, lift our hands, clasp our hands and rave or boast as expressions of His overwhelming grace in our lives. A song is nothing more than a means of uniting our focus. A song gives us the same lyric to the same tempo to the same rhythm to the same beat to the same Lord at the same time. It would be impossible for us to accomplish that without the use of rhythm. We can accomplish rhythm without aggression, but its time we understand God desires aggressive praise and worship. We need to be freed in our own hearts from the lie that rhythm and volume are from the devil. Another word for volume is amplitude. We must understand that amplitude determines attitude, and attitude determines our altitude in praise. We need to make a united, joyful noise unto the Lord. Lift up our voices! Get in rhythm with the heartbeat of God.

There must be a dramatic change in the sound in the house of the Lord. In many cultures we have adopted a nice, acceptable, palatable sound of worship, marketable to our musical preferences. I dare say God is even going to change our musical preferences. God's about to put some grit back into it. David danced before the Lord with *all* his might. He looked like seventeen cheerleaders in one body heading up that nine-mile road from Obed-Edom's house to Mount Zion in front of the ark. It says he praised the Lord, dancing with all his might. If you danced for nine miles, it would be all of your might, too!

God desires to release a sound that our petty issues cannot resist. Where's the best place in the world to hide from God? In the church. The number one reason people don't go to church is because they've already been, and there isn't anything there that impacts them and brings freedom to their lives. They see it as just another social event requiring time, energy, and money if they get involved. Many people hide in the church simply by dealing with their personal guilt issues from a religious mind-set. But the sound God desires to release will chase religion from the church and bring truth. He desires the sound of many waters, the sound of mighty thunder, and the sound of His glory and authority in the church.

It's time to use drums in intercession to call out to the Spirit of God to smite our enemies. In Isaiah 30, the Lord spoke of His judgment against Assyria, the enemy nation of Israel. Verse 31-32 says, *"For through the voice of the Lord Assyria will be beaten down, as He strikes the rod. And in every place where the staff of punishment passes, which the Lord lays on him, it will be with tambourines and harps; and in battles of brandishing He will fight with it."* The Israelites defeated the enemy by literally smiting their tambourines and harps. The word used for tambourine is *tohph*, meaning "drum, timbrel, or tabret." Using the rhythm of God they warred with instruments using the same passion and aggression with which they worshiped.

I believe one of the reasons rhythm is such an issue in the church today is because the world has so effectively used music with aggressive rhythms and beats. We've seen its impact on people living rebellious lives. The rebellion has offended us to the point that we've become accustomed to rejecting the sound. Many have never been exposed to an effective use of aggressive music, rhythms, or beats with Godly purposes. We need to quit being offended *by* it and start offending the enemy *with* it. According to Scripture as we submit to God, He will strike our enemies with the rod. *"In every place where the staff of punishment passes, Which the Lord lays on him, It will be with tambourines tabrets, timbrels and drums"* (Isaiah 30:32). To offend requires that we get on the offensive. Let's give up our defensive positions and march to the cadence of the Spirit of God. May the sound of our drums come into agreement with the mighty thunder of worship in heaven. Then the storms and wind of the Spirit will be released to free us from the slavery the enemy intends for us. May our worship become the "warship" that carries us to victory as we restore the treasures that rightfully belong to a people of truth. May we never again be victims or slaves to our enemies, but be a people who can truly say, *"Blessed are the people who know the joyful sound!"* (Psalm 89:15)

Chapter Eleven

Leaving Egypt with a New Sound

God desires to release a new sound free from man's oppression, just as He did through His chosen people Israel as they came out of Egypt. Israel was in bondage to Egypt, and they could not worship while in bondage to man. Exodus 5:1 says Moses and Aaron told Pharaoh, *"Thus says the Lord God of Israel: 'Let my people go, that they may hold a feast to Me in the wilderness.'"* In verse 3, the issue of conflict is spelled out again when Moses and Aaron said, *"The God of the Hebrews has met with us. Please let us go three days journey into the desert and sacrifice to the Lord our God."* In verse 8, the children of Israel were crying out, *"Let us go and sacrifice to our God."* Freedom of worship was the issue that led them to fight for their freedom.

If you study the original Hebrew writings, you'll find that during the 400 years of Israel's physical and spiritual bondage, their music was also in bondage. Scholars and linguists say the inflections of the Hebrew language at that time were marked in such a way to give us understanding of the variation of notes, tones, and melodies of the Hebrew people.

There were only three notes in what we understand today to be their musical scale. Keep in mind, music is always an expression of the state of man's mind and spirit. The three notes found in their writings during those 400 years were of a minor mode composing a hauntingly morbid sound. Their music reflected their depression and bondage. It was "mashing-out-mud-and-making-bricks-music," that was saturated with depression. As a result of Moses' and Aaron's persistence in declaring God's desire to Pharaoh, God miraculously performed all the plagues and disasters against Egypt. Pharaoh finally gave in. God completely healed each of the children of Israel. Psalm 105:37-38 says that there was not one sick or feeble person among them and that all of Egypt, plagued with disease and sickness as a result of God's hand against it, was glad to see them go.

The children of Israel soon realized that even though they were freed from their enemies, it did not keep them from being pursuing by them, and pursue they did, right into the Red Sea. When the children of Israel walked across the Red Sea and looked back to see their enemies utterly destroyed, something phenomenal took place. They all received immediate deliverance from the fear of their enemy, and their music came into agreement with this miracle. Suddenly, Miriam grabbed her tambourine—her hand drum, if you will—and said, "C'mon, girls! *Sing to the Lord, For He has triumphed gloriously! The horse and its rider, He has thrown into the sea!*" (Exodus 15:20) They sang twenty-one verses and danced with their timbrels and tambourines. Right there, within those twenty-one verses, their music was changed into a full scale of notes, with movement, melody, joy, and victory that had not been heard in the people of God for 400 years. They gained their freedom to worship God, and their music reflected it. As God brought them into a new freedom, they brought forth the new sound.

Worshipping in Bondage

Bondage can be blatant or it can be subtle and deceptive. In America, the land of the free, and the home of the brave, we have been given permission even in our Constitution to worship God in our own way. We can all truly thank God for that. But let me say that Scripture never tells us we can worship God in our own way. We are not to worship God in *our* own way. We are to worship Him in *His* own way. Scripture clearly spells out that we are to worship Him according to His word, His instruction and His way. If man was left to worship God in his own way, he simply would not worship Him. He would create numerous rules, regulations, stipulations and religious hoops to jump through in his quest to find some intellectually stimulating way to put God in a box. This would diminish the purity of heartfelt worship to a religious ritual.

Throughout history, we have simply not had the revelation that we have today in personal or corporate worship. In light of the revelation that's come to the body of Christ in the last generation, we can look back at some of the religious antics and ideas we've embraced and have a good laugh, or perhaps a good cry. An interesting example of our embrace of the absurd came when the Quakers settled in Pennsylvania. At the time, there was much controversy and division regarding what man thought was musically acceptable to God in the church. The Quakers resisted music along with other things they opposed, such as plays, games, and dancing. This attitude was a marked contrast to the members of the Church of England who consistently championed light amusements and favored music. The Germans and the Swedes who settled in the neighborhood of Philadelphia used vocal and instrumental music at that time. They attached such a priority to music in the church that one pastor of a Swedish church imposed a fine of six shillings upon certain members of his congregation for what he called "untimely singing." But none of these groups gave much attention to the reality of music being a heartfelt expression of intimacy or worship to God. It was strictly a religious rite.

A group of Germans called the Pietists, who came to America for religious reasons, also settled near Philadelphia. They brought instruments with them and accompanied their hymn singing with instrumental music. They offended many in their day with their use of the trumpet, viol, hautboy (oboe), and a kettle drum. Another group of Germans settled west of Philadelphia at Ephratah. One of its leaders devised a very interesting and peculiar type of music. He took his ideas from nature and tried to represent the Aeolian harp by means of harmony of voices. An Aeolian harp is a thin-sounding box with strings that are played by the wind. In the group's music, the voices of the choir imitated soft instrumental music.

The music was set in two, four, five, and seven parts. All the parts except the bass were sung by women's voices. The bass was set in two parts, the high and low bass, with the latter resembling the deep tones of an organ. The melody was sung with falsetto voice, and the singers were disallowed to open their mouths or move their lips. It's said that the effect produced by this peculiar technique of singing made it seem like the music entered the room from above in some mysterious way and hovered over the heads of the audience. The mysterious sound gave them some sense of awe in an attempt to introduce a mystical presence in the service. They embraced the pietistic notion that if any attention was given to the performance of the music, God would be displeased. Needless to say, this practice didn't last very long, so this guy was canned for being a little too weird. But it demonstrates man's desire to find ways to express his worship. Unfortunately, he didn't always use solid theology and Scriptural justification. Just as it is today, I'm sure there were many church squabbles and heated debates on how to worship God. Unfortunately, controversy and conflict have always given way to strife and anger, therefore diminishing unity. I believe the real key to corporate worship is unity brought about by corporate humility.

If we're constantly fighting for position to worship God in our own ways, God will never be worshiped in the way He desires. If we give all attention to the "how-to" worship and no attention to the "Who-to" worship, we're in trouble. However, Scripture has given us guidelines and clarity on the "how" if we genuinely desire the "Who." The "how" of worship is an inexhaustible subject with literally infinite possibilities. He is an infinite God. If we can simply agree with the wonderful drama of worship taking place in heaven, we'll find that worship is not nearly as weird or boring as man has made it in his search to put God in his religious boxes. God truly desires a people to worship Him, to come out of the slavery and bondage to man. We give our life energy to mashing out mud and making bricks to the tune of three mundane notes. God desires for us to step across the Red Sea and give birth to a new sound from heaven.

Worship in the Early Church

There are periods in history where sparse light and revelation were brought forth. These times were called the Dark Ages. I propose there have been many times in history of "dark ages" with regards to music and sound. Into such a season, Jesus was born. The night the heavenly choir and the burst of light jolted the universe with the sound of heaven, the sound rang out to a world full of misery. There was constant warfare between the powerful Roman empire and the many barbaric tribes such as the Teutonic (German), Celtic (Irish), Norse (Danish, Swedish, and Norwegian) and Gallic (French). All of these nations and tribes were fighting for existence, developing into the nations we know today. Julius Caesar had just completed a season of invading the entire world as best he could. This was a world of selfishness, with little love for humanity, little sympathy for the downtrodden and unhappy, few kind words for the

115

poor and sick, very little justice and even less mercy. In the middle of that dark world, the Light of the World came with a song.

A few hundred years after the time of Jesus, the world went through one of these periods called the Dark Ages. We might ask how it could have been any darker than the time prior to Jesus' birth. But this period was ushered in by the fall of the Roman Empire around A.D. 476. Rome, the city of glorious victories and advanced culture, became the prey of barbaric tribes such as the Huns, Goths, Visigoths, Vandals, Franks, Saxons, and Slavs, until it seemed that civilization would be wiped out and people would become primitive again. But during these early centuries, music was saved by a small band of faithful followers of Jesus. Jesus Himself was brought up in the religion of the Hebrews and on many occasions we find Him singing the songs of His father David. The beautiful musical tradition of the Jewish race found its way into the services of the early Christian church since those early believers were well acquainted with Hebrew beliefs. Following this, the Hebrew Bible text was translated into Latin, the everyday language of the Romans. Since most of the early Christians lived in Rome, they followed the rules of music the Romans learned from the Greeks. So our church music of today was influenced by both Hebrews and Greeks.

For about three hundred years, the early Christians had to hold their services in secret because they were punished even by death for worshiping any god but Jupiter and other Roman gods. The Christians were not the rich and influential people of the day. They were simply humble folks who embraced with their whole hearts the teachings of Jesus. They had no beautiful palaces in which to hold services. They were hiding from the Roman centurions, so they worshiped in dark, secret places without musical instruments so as not to attract the attention of the enemy. Needless to say, it was a season in history where music had a hard time just staying alive. From what we gather, the early Christians chanted their songs much as the Hebrews did. As time progressed, emperors like Constantine began to take away the death penalty for believing in Jesus. One of the main reasons for this serves as a powerful testimony to the power of worship. Christians were frequently thrown to the lions as a source of Roman entertainment. The Christians believed deeply in their hearts in worshiping God with song. As the lions rushed into the arena to devour them, they would stand boldly and lift their voices and sing praises to their God. These songs were so powerful and anointed, the violent roar from the crowd turned into a hush so the lyrics could be heard. As time after time these Christians would be thrown to the lions only to release a song before their death, it became such a moving and awesome scene that it simply lost the sense of victory and sport for the barbaric audience.

During the early days of such martyrdom, thousands of Christians faced the horrors of this kind of death. But out of these harsh and primitive times, music began to have seasons of growth and development. In one sense man was leaving the Dark Ages. Yet in another, he was merely walking into the next, even darker age, as Roman and Greek ways of thinking began to dominate the Hebrew mind set, giving way for idolatry to become part of Christian worship. In Exodus 20:4 God forbade the Hebrews to make images: *"You shall not make for yourself a carved image–any likeness of anything that is in heaven above, or that is in the earth beneath, or that is in the water under the earth."* With such a strict command, it's understandable why there aren't many pictures of singers and instruments from the days of the Hebrew prophets. But along with the Roman influence, the face of Christianity changed as the Greeks brought their mythology and idolatry into worship. To this day, some religious denominations embrace an unhealthy attraction to idols and graven images that have been incorporated into what they consider Christian worship.

Music in Hebrew history also developed during the early days when people wandered from place to place as shepherd tribes. Their only meeting house was a tent. Their music was simple but extremely expressive and demonstrative. Moses was quite learned in music, as he had been educated in Pharaoh's household. He learned music from Egyptian priests. As the Hebrews were led by Moses, they adopted the Egyptian customs concerning instruments in the making of their own. An example would be when Moses received the command from God to make two silver trumpets. If God was going to tell him to build a trumpet, he had to have some point of reference.

Throughout history, whether it is ancient biblical history or recent history from last week, man and his music have been in a constant state of development and change. But one thing has been true in every time period: We have been ever seeking to worship God. This is why we were created. If we are not worshipers of God, we have forfeited our reason for existence. Through the ages, man has clumsily stumbled in and out of every imaginable spiritual calisthenics in his quest to worship God.

Musical transformation throughout history was brought about by man's desire to worship. This is one of the reasons I believe David has become the model for our worship. He simply worshiped God with all his heart, and with all his might. Everything within him came bursting forth in passionate worship. His focus was not how to worship. His focus was truly the "Who" that he worshiped. Therefore, his life, with all its strengths and weaknesses, victories and defeats, became a pattern for the people of God in his day, while his songs became a lyric for generations. That's why the Word prophetically declares in the last days God *"will rebuild the tabernacle of David which has fallen down. I will rebuild its ruins, And I will set it up, So that the rest of mankind may seek the Lord"* (Acts 15:16-17).

Those ruins separate us from priority one, which is seeking the Lord. They can be walls of religion, unsanctified ambition, ungodly desire, strife or walls of idolatry. They can even be walls built of the timbers from the tree of knowledge of good and evil. Knowledge can be the greatest enemy of truth. The great desire of God's heart is a people who will worship Him in spirit and truth, not from the mind. May we step out of our personal dark ages into truth and light.

119

Chapter Twelve

The Sound of War

There are at least twenty different types of songs recorded in the Bible, from songs of praise to songs of harlots and drunkards. One type of song worthy of note is the war song. Every nation seems to produce most of its songs during times of conflict. More songs were written during and immediately after America's Civil War than any other time in our nation's history. One of the reasons for this is because music at that time was the primary means of communicating the news of the day. But the romantic, melancholy songs of wartime are not the subjects here. The focus is the role the song, or the sound, actually played in times of war.

Many instruments from virtually every part of the globe have played an important role in battle. As stated previously, many times the trumpet was used, and in more modern times, the bugle was used. During the Revolutionary War, the fife and drum alerted the enemy that they were about to be attacked. What an amazing concept! "Let us play the fife and drum and make all the noise possible to inform our enemy we're coming toward them." So much for surprise attack! Why did the buglers of the cavalry see it necessary to release the blast and provoke the charge? What sometimes seems to be so obvious often has some very pertinent hidden nuggets that we overlook.

A Worshiping William Wallace

Most of us had never heard of William Wallace until the 1995 film *Braveheart*, starring Mel Gibson, which overtook America's screens. I had the privilege of traveling to Scotland and doing in-depth research on this great warrior. I found many interesting facts that didn't make it to Hollywood. Though much of the movie's account was historically accurate, I'd like to give you a slightly different version, which includes some hidden history of the battles of William Wallace. And I ask you to please not take offense if you are British. History teaches that the British ruthlessly oppressed many nations over the years. The offended have been slow to forget. Yet, how quickly we forget that some of the greatest preachers and missionaries in history made their way to the four corners of the earth from England's shores. Sometimes we fail to see the light that they brought to the nations and focus on the darkness. Truly this was a time of darkness and oppression.

William Wallace was born near Paisley, Scotland, to Sir Malcolm Wallace, a small-land owner. His family, probably of Norman descent, was not wealthy, and William had none of the advantages of the ruling elite of the day. He was taught the usual marshal skills and apparently, even as a youngster, showed great promise as he wielded the sword and claymore. His skill proved quite useful in the years ahead. He became an expert hunter. While William was still young, his father was killed by the English as they oppressed Scotland. Fatherless, Wallace was then raised and educated by clerics. He was daily taught the Word of God and had a particular love for the Psalms. The priests who raised him instilled in him a strong sense of freedom. It was said he particularly loved the story of King David and considered him to be the greatest Jewish freedom fighter of all time. Wallace memorized the entire book of Psalms by heart, which became the greatest inspiration in his struggles for his nation.

He was a young man of God who easily reconciled violence and piety. In the thirteenth century, "might" usually meant "right." The theological argument was that strength was given to those who "deserved" it. Physical bravery was a virtue in itself, and courage was synonymous with faith. They believed victors had the support of the angels, while the defeated were often considered too weak of character to triumph. It was a very Old Testament view of life, with little room for love and grace. Times were hard and produced hard men. However, even in the midst of his most violent campaigns, Wallace would find time to sneak away to churches and take part in the services. He carried a psalter, or the book of Psalms, everywhere he went. Before his greatest battles, these songs gave him comfort as well as the inspiration he would need to release the fury of his heart upon his enemies. Prior to battle, he would gather his followers together and preach the Word of God in such a way to impart fire to their souls and courage to their hearts. This same mentality led to the formation of warrior monks like the Templars and the Hospitalers, who saw no contradiction in combining their fighting skills with their deep Christian faith.

William grew into a giant of a figure. Even as a young man, he stood six feet and seven inches tall. He was muscular and strong with unbelievable endurance in battle. He had nothing going for him politically, no wealth, and no military budget. Instead he relied upon his physical attributes, strength and his deep belief that God's justice would bring him forth as a victor. The declining state of his country, and the harsh injustices imposed upon the poor by the ruthless and barbaric bondage of English oppression continually furthered Wallace's incentive to fight. Because his father had died fighting the English, William had been forced into a life of exile. In his desperate and brooding heart, he felt he had to take some kind of action. All things considered, he had nothing to lose. At every opportunity he single-handedly confronted English soldiers and miraculously overcame his enemies, though he was sometimes outnumbered fifteen to one. He was like a fighting machine as he wielded his claymore of five feet eight inches. He made a profound impression on many of the oppressed young locals, and they decided they would create a small band of warriors to fight for the cause. There was much talk among them about forming a strategy for expelling the English.

One day, while in the village, a garrison of English soldiers challenged young William. In a split-second, out of nowhere, he whirled his ferocious sword and sliced off the arm of his opponent before anyone had time to react. William and his companions, vastly outnumbered by reinforcements arriving by the minute, managed to escape leaving more than fifty dead or wounded behind. They fled to William's house and then out a back garden gate into the open countryside and into the hills. The soldiers arrived outside of William's house, where his wife Marion waited. They demanded she hand over Wallace, but she blatantly defied them, barred the door and shouted at them from an upstairs window, giving William and his comrades time to make good his escape. The soldiers smashed in the door and stormed the house. When they realized she had been stalling, the sheriff ordered Marion executed on the spot. Her dying words were in defiance to Scotland's oppressors.

When William heard about the murder of his wife, he took his psalter and went away in solitude and grief. After dark, Wallace's small group of men wandered back into the town, some were disguised as monks. The English troops, believing their hunted outlaws were far away, paid little attention to these stragglers–not even to the large monster of a figure dressed like a monk. William walked straight to the sheriff's house and in one blow burst the door in, bolted up the stairs and executed immediate vengeance upon the murderer of his bride. It didn't stop there. Before the night was over, the streets ran red with the blood of the English. One hundred died that night. Only women, children, and priests were spared. News of this event spread like a wildfire across Scotland as a signal to the oppressed that a revolt had begun. Suddenly Wallace's picture was on every post office wall in the land. The capture of Wallace was now top priority for the English army. As this news spread through the villages of Scotland, old and young men alike believed this incident showed that God did not appear to be on the side of the English, since He did not protect them from Wallace. His name was spoken of in every tavern across the land as a folk hero and leader of the day. This young, heartbroken, exiled, outlawed warrior burning with anger, was ready to take on all the might King Edward could throw at him.

Wallace soon found himself to be the commander of a raw, impoverished, desperate army of highlanders carrying sticks, rocks, rusty battle axes, hunting spears, and homemade swords. They possessed a fire in their desperate hearts to see their enemies utterly destroyed. Wallace had never imagined himself as the leader of an army. He was simply fighting out of desperation, principle, and a sense of justice. Now he found himself having to address the issues of the day from a political position as well as being a military strategist. The clansmen who had gravitated to him were nothing more than a ragtag bunch of farmers and sheep herders with a common dream of freedom. William led them north into the highlands where Andrew deMoray, a young knight as wild and vicious as Wallace, was raising up mounted troops of Gaels. Together, under Wallace's leadership, they began terrorizing the English. They established a network of spies to keep them informed of English activity. They began attacking English outposts and garrisons and even stormed entire cities. William led an attack on Glasgow, and as he headed his men up High Street, he ordered them to "stock well the Clyde River with English soldiers." This command is commemorated to this day in the name of Stockwell Street, which leads down to the river.

The English army that faced Wallace was known as the greatest fighting machine of its age. It consisted of proud knights in their finest armor. Their huge war horses wore fancy harnesses. The knights were all decked out in colorful finery with banners hanging from every lance, shield, and ornament that glistened in the sun. It was an army that had never known defeat. The Scots, in contrast, were a bunch of ill-disciplined, poorly-armed, ragged men with homemade weapons. They came down the hills in their rough tunics carrying supplies of oats, lentils and bags over their shoulders. But they had God and Wallace, and for them that was enough. For years, they had suffered under the English burden, and now it was time to strike back and free their country. A showdown was imminent.

A Sound of Death

On September 10, 1297, the stage was set at Sterling Bridge. The English forces sent a messenger to the Scots demanding they submit or else. William looked down the mountain at the thousands of glittering spears held by foot-soldiers and, knowing he was outnumbered ten to one, told the messenger, "Tell your people we have not come here to gain peace but for battle, to avenge and deliver our country. Let them come up when they like and they will find us ready to meet them to their beards." In other words, we'll be in their faces.

From the hilltops that evening at sundown, the eerie sound of a primitive version of the Highland pipes began to screech and moan across the valley. The sound of the wardrums began to thunder, announcing to its hearer's bloodshed was sure. Remember, these highlanders are believed to descendants of the warring Celts and Picts, both known for their vicious tenacity in war. Their military conduct was like nothing you would see at West Point.

In the movie *Braveheart,* do you remember when they painted their faces blue and white, decorating themselves with what we think of as Indian war paint? That's not the way it was in the days of the Celts and Picts. They painted their entire bodies from head to foot with this sky blue paste and covered their hair with white ashes. I guess you could say they looked like really mean Smurfs. They didn't wear kilts in battle, either. As a matter of fact, in one sweeping motion, they would throw off their kilts, tunics or whatever they wore. With a violent battle cry, they corporately shouted and screamed as they charged their enemy. It was a massive mobilization of terror on foot. They would completely abandon themselves to the fight. It was extremely effective for introducing fear to the enemy before the actual physical attack.

Probably the most effective tactic used in that type of warfare took place at the beginning of sundown the night before battle. Huge bonfires were built and massive drums maintained a steady rumble of beats throughout the night, while the screeching of the pipes would permeate the ears and minds of the enemy. The pipes were a warring instrument. It was a sound used even in David's time. As David's musicians would release a death-nell selah on the enemy of Israel, the moans and groans of the reed pipes would pronounce judgment and death. Fear would grip the hearts of the enemy of Israel's God, for that sound declared God was going to war on behalf of His people. The reputation of God to those heathen and pagan nations was that He was an awesome God able to break down walls and drown entire Egyptian armies in the Red Sea. Now get this: Low frequencies cause a physical response in the circulatory system of the body. High frequencies cause a response in the nervous system. That's one of the reasons extremely high sounds get on your nerves. High screaming tones can put your teeth on edge. Certain low frequencies can literally stop your heart.

At sundown, Wallace's army began to release the low thundering sounds and frequencies that were, if not physically, at least mentally impacting their enemy. The sound sent out the message that hearts would stop beating and bloodshed would be a reality. The high frequencies screeched and moaned out the sad, dissonant sound. Needless to say, after a few hours, these unending notes would get on your nerves. I don't use the word "unending" loosely, for a bagpipe is an instrument that has been created to sustain a note forever. You can sustain a note on a bagpipe until a tree dies somewhere, because it has its own lung. The bag is a reservoir of air that continues to blow a continuous note while the player has opportunity to breathe. Imagine that you're one of those English soldiers camping down in the valley while your enemy is bombarding you with these eerie sounds. These are sounds of aggression, fear, and the sadness of death. Imagine Wallace gathering his men before daybreak, calling the musicians to silence as he opens the psalter and soberly brings the Word of God. He reminds all that *"if God be for us, who can be against us?"* (Romans 8:31 KJV) Even as David slew thousands for the purpose of freeing God's people from the bondage of man, so we will come forth victorious as our God fights for us and with us. As he prays a prayer of blessing and protection over them, a signal from his lookout informs them the English are beginning to move.

At dawn, five thousand English foot-soldiers began crossing the bridge as Wallace and his men moved into position for an all-out attack. As the sun began to peak over that valley it shone on the painted faces of a determined army. Wallace ordered his spear-men to hold their ground until they heard his horn, which only he was allowed to blow, and then to charge forward down the hill. As the English army made its way over the wooden bridge, Wallace and his men viewed the slow movement of their forces from a high vantage point. This must have been an awesome sight, seeing the ranks of their enemies swell below them, yet keeping calm with ears tuned in anticipation of the blast of Wallace's horn. Wallace knew that a premature move would be destructive for his small band of warriors. The English viewed his hesitancy and inaction as cowardly. They were anxious to charge, even though only half of their men had crossed over the river. Suddenly, before the English could fully ready themselves for a charge, Wallace judged that enough of the enemy was spread below him as to give him the perfect opportunity for his attack. He gave a mighty blast on his horn and the Scots surged down upon their enemy, yelling their blood-curdling war cries and screaming their way toward the bridge. Wallace, with his massive sword in hand, declared Psalm 91 over his enemies. The bridge was long and narrow, only wide enough to allow horses to cross two by two. With half of the foot soldiers on one side of the river, half on the other, and the bridge clogged with the mounted soldiers in all their armor, chaos ruled the English army. Four hundred knights and archers and five thousand foot-soldiers lost their lives. No prisoners were taken, while Scottish losses were negligible.

As horrible as this may sound (and you must remember the day and time I'm speaking of), the English leader was killed and skinned. To this day, his flesh provides the leather for the handle of Wallace's sword, where it is encased at the William Wallace monument that stands on a mountain overlooking the scene of the Battle of Sterling Bridge. From that victory many others came, until finally the English were able to overwhelm Wallace as a result of betrayal in Wallace's own camp.

We can learn much from Wallace's story. Sound has always been and always will be one of the most important forces God ever created. Simple sound can give way to every imaginable emotion. It can calm our souls at the side of a brook as we hear water trickling over small stones. It can utterly frighten us in an instant as a tray of dishes are dropped in a restaurant. Sound can soothe the weary mind to a place of sleep and rest. Sound can cause the earth to convulse in the form of an earthquake. An earthquake is nothing more than sound modulations between two layers of stone formations that can be miles under the earth. Windows can be blown out of your house as airplanes break the sound barrier. Nerves can be put on edge at the sound of the monotonous dripping of a faucet. Man can be motivated by the sound of a song to give his life for his country. Man can be motivated by the sound of enticing words to betray a Godly marriage and carry out lustful and sinful acts. We can swell with pride at the sound of an anthem being played as our sons and daughters walk down the aisle with tasseled caps. We can be jolted into action at the sound of a fire alarm, or we can be lulled to sleep at the whisper of a breeze.

The movie *Braveheart* depicted the scene where young William Wallace had just received the news that his father was dead. His aged, old uncle had come to take him home. The scene was sad and moving as   a piper played a mournful song in the moonlight. The young boy questioned the old man about the piper. The old man simply said, "He's playing an outlawed song on outlawed pipes." The reason pipes and songs were outlawed was because they stirred such national sentiment and memories of better days. The piper reminded them of a simpler time without the harsh, oppressing, malicious presence of English rule. So in times of battle, those pipes and songs would stir up loyalty, strength, unity

131

and national pride. The pipes meant disloyalty to the throne of England. In order for England to bring them into bondage, their music had to be in bondage as well. At one point, England confiscated all the pipes and drums they could find and burned them in huge bonfires. Let me ask you, was the strength of the army in the drum? Was the strength of the army in the pipe? Was the strength of the army found in the blasting horn or the shout? No. These were simply exterior sounds depicting the inner heart attitude. The instruments provided a means for the heart to be expressed.

Is there a particular anointing on instruments or sounds today that will give us the upper hand on our enemies? Yes and no. Yes, because particular sounds, tones, and frequencies motivate us to particular responses. And no, because an instrument does not have a life of its own. It is an inanimate object. However, God can use inanimate objects to do miraculous things. Remember what happened when the hem of the garment of Jesus was touched? Remember what happened when the inanimate stone hit Goliath between the eyes?

A lifeless musical instrument is nothing more than a tool used for the expression of one that does have life. There's nothing more holy in a Martin guitar than there is in a Gibson guitar. However, different sounds demand different actions. Different rhythms promote different attitudes. Different melodies and harmonies bring forth different emotions. Various lyrics create entirely different images causing us to have a united focus in corporate praise and worship.

When we sing the word "freedom" in a congregational song with a heartfelt release of faith, it can be as powerful as David's stone thrown at the head of the enemy. We should have faith for that. After all, how many Bible stories do we have to hear before we'll start believing God desires us to be free? Freedom from the bondage of sin and the curse of the enemy was the very issue which brought Jesus to mankind. Since the garden, Satan has tried to use man to implement his desires and enslave us in every arena of life. Satan knows if he can enslave one man he can potentially use that man to enslave others.

Through the ages, history records that men have always desired to dominate one another on every level. Man is engaged in a continual struggle to be king of the mountain. If one kingdom can overcome another with ungodly authority, it is then able to enjoy the intoxication of power for a season. Nations and kingdoms gain a sense of power as a result of taking peoples and lands through domination and slavery. Most of the time it is motivated out of a desire for riches. If you dominate the people, your reward is resources. If I own the land, I own the gold, oil, timber, and water, and I control the people to harvest all those resources. That gives me power and wealth. God sent His Son to introduce mankind to His purpose for authority while combating the perversion of authority by domination and greed. When Jesus came, He said, *"If anyone desires to be first, he shall be last of all and servant of all"* (Mark 9:35). The Bible also declares *"if the Son makes you free, you shall be free indeed"* (John 8:36). God desires us to be free from every bondage of the enemy. There is another example given about freedom brought about through praise and worship. I'm sure you know the story.

When God Sings Bass

Paul and Silas walked into town. They had come to spread the gospel in Rome. Everywhere Paul and Silas went, they wound up in jail! An evangelist today checks out the Holiday Inns and the Marriotts when he comes into town. I imagine Paul and Silas checked out the local jail when they came into town. They knew they'd wind up there sooner or later before they left! The Bible says they were walking down the street going to pray somewhere and ran into a woman possessed by a spirit of divination (Acts 16: 16). For many days this loudmouthed woman followed them around declaring, *"These men are the servants of the Most High God, who proclaim to us the way of salvation"* (verse 17). Paul finally had all he could take, and being grieved by this spirit of divination, though it was speaking truth, turned and said to the spirit, *"I command you in the name of Jesus Christ to come out of her"* (verse 18). And it did. When her master saw that Paul had just torn up his meal ticket (she was a demonic moneymaking machine for him), he and his men caught Paul and Silas and dragged them to the rulers at the marketplace. He declared to the magistrates, *"These men, being Jews, exceedingly trouble our city; and they teach customs which are not lawful for us, being Romans, to receive or observe"* (verses 20-21). The whole crowd rose up against them. The magistrates ripped Paul and Silas' clothes off and had them beaten and thrown into the inner prison. They were in what we would consider a maximum security cell, with their feet in stocks chained to the wall. The citizens and magistrates believed that to maintain their lifestyles and laws, they had to bring Paul and Silas into bondage.

Paul and Silas lay in the darkness of this cell at midnight, praying and singing to God. The prisoners were listening to them. Did you know you cannot pray or sing to God without Him getting involved? You know God loves a concert. While Paul and Silas were singing praises, God heard the prayers of these two righteous men and gave His attention to the expression of their hearts. Picture God sitting on His throne, and enjoying the song they were singing. He begins to tap His foot. Then He begins to hum. Then He begins to sing, and God sings bass, you know. In Zephaniah 3:17, it says *"He will rejoice over you with singing."* Well, when God began to sing, it was such a powerful low frequency that in Acts 16:26 it says, *"Suddenly there was a great earthquake, so that the foundations of the prison were shaken; and immediately all the doors were opened and everyone's chains were loosed."*

Now imagine that. As a result of a simple song of praise, God performed the miraculous. You know He loves to do that! They were suddenly released from the bondage placed upon them by man. The keeper of the prison was awakened out of a deep sleep to see the prison doors open. The very man oppressing them now drew his sword to commit suicide. Those who are so quick to ridicule the praise and worship of others, who consider others to be too weird or too heavenly

135

minded to be any earthly good, are prime candidates for experiencing a spiritual earthquake. In one traumatic moment, the sneer of God can turn into the fear of God. Let tragedy hit where they live and they'll do just as this jailer did. Unable to cope with this catastrophe, he went running to Paul and Silas and fell down trembling before them. Remember this: At any given moment, you can have people trembling on your porch looking for answers, and looking for life. They might be just like the jailer who cried out, *"Sirs, what must I do to be saved?"* (verse 30)

I believe the number one tool of evangelism in the earth today is praise. Out of praise, a sound is released that *suddenly* shakes the chains of our bondage and grabs the attention of the lost around us. For instance, the night the church was born in the upper room, while they were praying and worshiping God, another *suddenly* happened. For suddenly, the Spirit of the Lord came upon them as a *sound* of a rushing mighty wind. Later, as that sound was noised abroad in the streets, thousands were added daily to the church. The jailer who gave his heart to the Lord witnessed his entire family being saved that very night because he took Paul and Silas home with him. He washed their stripes and ministered to their needs. Paul and Silas baptized his entire family. When the magistrates heard about all of this, their attitude changed from aggressive superiority to subtle arrogance. They sent officers to give the jailer a message: *"Let those men go"* (Acts 16:35). The jailer should have sent a message back, saying, "God has already done that." Imagine the presumption of those magistrates assuming they could let these men go. Pride really is something, isn't it?

Whether you find yourself in the grips of political and national oppression or simply dominated by the oppressive personality of your neighbor, oppression is still oppression. Bondage is still bondage. William Wallace cried out his dying words in the faces of his oppressors who insisted he yield to their throne, at his shout of the word "freedom," he truly experienced it. His cry for freedom took him to heaven, where he found it. May we be a people with such power, prayer, and praise that we can bring heaven to us. May our shouts shake the very foundation of every prison we find ourselves in, break the chains of bondage and cause the nations to tremble at the Word of the Lord. God grant us the authority in the spirit realm to touch heaven, and that the sound of heaven would be heard in the earth.

If your oppressors try to storm the battlefield of your mind, or break your body down with disease, you can defy them in the spirit realm with praise. All depression, despondency, and despair will flee. Like David, lift up a shout and watch your enemies flee a thousand ways.

Chapter Thirteen

The Sound of Heaven, A People of Praise

America is a concentrated nucleus of the world's sounds. All the different ethnic and cultural sounds can be found here in America because each culture brought their sounds with them. Every nation in this world has its own folk dance and its own national anthem. Particular tones and timbres have been given to every nation. Every nation has a sound that causes a response in the spirits of individuals born into that culture. There's a common thread in the nature of every black man on earth that makes him respond to certain tones and rhythms. Every Irishman on earth has that common element in his nature that makes him respond when he hears the pipes played. Every culture and ethnic group have things that cause a response by their spirits. No one on this earth was born without a spirit. Because music is a force, God created it to open the spirit of every person. There is no living or breathing creation of God that will not respond to music. Man has been given the sole opportunity to use that as an act of intimacy and worship with God.

There is an element and a part of God's divine nature He placed in us that He didn't place in any other form of creation. It's His divine attribute of creativity.

Musicians have a common thread directly linked to the creative nature of God. Lucifer, in his jealousy, has tried to sow such calamities, confusion and deception into every creative person. Satan, the fallen chief musician, steals, kills, and destroys by using the very thing that gives us an audience with God—music (see John 10:10). Lucifer covets the position he had. His name was *"anointed cherub who covers"* the throne of God (see Ezekiel 28:14). When he was cast down, he left the throne uncovered. When he was created, in his very being was created the sound of all instruments (see Isaiah 14:11 and Ezekiel 28:13). He held within him the sound of the piano, flute, guitar, drums, pipes, and organ. All sound was created in him as part of his voice and music. He breathed notes. When he was cast down, he perverted those sounds, trying to use them to fulfill his vision for every man's life, which is to *"steal, and to kill, and to destroy"* (John 10:10 NIV).

When Satan left the throne uncovered, I believe God said, "I will create a people that will be a holy habitation for My presence, and I will enthrone Myself in the praises of My people." The covering of God's throne that was once lost, is now being restored as He creates a generation that will show forth His praises— a generation that will walk in signs, wonders, and power. One of the signs and wonders released will be the sound of heaven, a sound that is seen and heard.

Once in recent years, I saw it suddenly rain inside a church building during worship. In another meeting, people throughout the congregation simultaneously heard the sounds of instruments not physically in the room. Once I was present with three thousand others when a cloud the size of a grand piano appeared on stage. I would say those were signs and wonders, wouldn't you? But all that is a rehearsal for God. All He's doing is creating a stirring hunger in us. Now is the season for the beginning of the release of those signs and wonders.

What the devil has meant for evil, God will use for good (see Genesis 50:20). Our very differences—the unique deposits in each ethnic group—are going to become one corporate sound joined with the angelic hosts of heaven, resonating the sound of heaven throughout the earth. God will take one of the strengths from each of those groups, though they are somewhat cross-pollinated, and blend them into a unified sound. Isaiah *"saw the Lord sitting on a throne, high and lifted up, and the train of His robe filled the temple"* (Isaiah 6:1). The train represents God's people who follow Him into His holy habitation by the power of praise and worship. We live in an extremely exciting time. Down through the years, the enemy has tried to rob every people group. But now in the last days what the devil has meant for evil, God will use for good, capitalizing on the diversity He has created in us.

The Irish Sound

More than a million Irish people flocked to the United States in the 1840s as a result of the Potato Famine. Lucky just to be alive following the excruciating journey across the Atlantic, the survivors were impoverished. Only their traditional sounds came with them. In the last few years, there has been a sweeping popularity and fascination with the Irish sound as seen and heard in such successes as *Braveheart*, *Titanic*, and *Riverdance*. Something comes alive in us when we hear the sound of these productions. It causes a response. Advertisers and promoters have used this stirring of emotions as an effective ploy to make money. But God created the Irish sound and desires to use it for His purposes now. At one time the traditional Irish dance was one with shoulders high, back straight. As the Irish were exiled from their land and came to America, the offspring of that prideful Irish dance was clogging. In the transition, the shoulders dropped and head lowered. The Scotch-Irish expression became individual. It was no longer a war dance, and no longer carried a sense of militancy. The people suffered such harsh conditions when they came to America that their dance turned into an inward, individual expression of clogging. Clogging was a part of the isolation, depression, and poverty of the Appalachian Mountains. The men were the only ones who danced, as it was forbidden for women to dance in public. That's why it was called "buck dancing." Though they danced in public, these old mountain men would never sing in their homes. Singing was the important job for mothers. As they washed clothes and did daily chores in the isolation of their mountain homes, they would sing all day to pass the traditions of their homeland to their children. They couldn't read or write, which meant they couldn't teach their kids the fading traditions through literacy. So they would sing the traditions to them. This was called "lilting," singing the diddly-diddly-doo kind of sound. The women sang the Irish and Scottish airs with a high, mournful sound poured into their spirits through the Irish fiddle and other such instruments. The mothers were the ones who put the song in their children. They grew up understanding that singing was what they heard from mama. From this tradition, the high lonesome sound was born with the moaning, groaning, and the bending of notes.

A Church without Instruments

As the militancy of the Irish dance was robbed from its people, so was the militancy and passionate aggression in church music. Through the years, it seems the church has been insensitive to the needs of the common people and their cultural expression, whether it is the music or the dance of the homeland. At times, the church has even aggressively resisted those cultural traditional expressions. For example, for many years the church imposed the belief that the fiddle was the devil's box. Because the church took the instruments out of the hands of musicians and threw them out, music was lost. The church went through hundreds of years of what you would call the musical dark ages. Huge organs filling half the room replaced the instruments. This one big machine produced the sound of an orchestra without the need for tolerating the pettiness and overly-sensitive nature of some needy musicians. The result was an entire group of people in the eleventh century called the goliards. The goliards were defrocked priests, minstrels, and poet-prophets that wound up in the streets as traveling minstrels and troubadours. Because they were no longer wanted or needed by the church, now all the acts of ministry and worship were taken completely away from the people. All that was left was the drone of liturgical chants. These chants took the creative expression out of the hearts of God's people. Worship now consisted of leaders lulling both God and His people to sleep.

Out of that time period came a very passive, feminine sound. The warrior heart and sound of music, as well as the individual expression, was lost. The religious world has depicted heaven as some "ooh-ah, Kumbayah," ethereal place where people spend thousands of years musically bored, while the world continually finds newfangled technologies and ideas for enjoyment. The truth is quite the opposite. If we look at the complacent and apathetic dullness of some religious music as a depiction of what heaven will be like, we must agree it's going to be a never-ending yawn. However, in Scripture we see quite a different picture of heaven. We find great rejoicing, thunderous praise, harpists harping, hosannas, hallelujahs, lifted voices, and joyful noise. There's only thirty minutes of silence in the eternal heaven, and that's just while the angels inhale! Then they unload for another one thousand years with all that's in them and all of creation joins in a terrific blast of sound. I believe it's going to be loud in heaven.

I used to think, "My goodness, after about ten thousand years of floating around on a cloud singing 'Kumbayah,' heaven's going to get a little boring!" I had this mental picture of walking into heaven and watching angels pass out twelve-string guitars. We'd all take these twelve-strings, harps, or whatever we would get and float around for another million years. That was my view of heaven and it seemed mighty boring to me. Now I realize it will never get boring in heaven because endless creativity is the very nature of God. The twenty-four choruses of musicians established in the tabernacle of David represent the twenty-four elders in the book of Revelation. I love those elders. Every time the elders are mentioned we find them on their faces worshiping God. I heard a man say one time, "It'll be worth it to go to heaven just to find a group of elders who will consistently worship God."

Why does it never get boring in heaven? Because just like in the tabernacle of David and the temple of Solomon, there is a continual, fresh new beginning. When we get to heaven and we begin to see God as He really is, about every hour on the hour throughout eternity, He will reveal a whole new dimension of His nature that we've never understood in earthly realms. It will always be exciting. Look at Revelation 4. Everything and everyone surrounding the throne of God is walking around in a daze. All they can say is, *"Holy! Holy! Holy!"* (verse 8). Why "holy?" Because as they behold each new part of God's nature for that one moment in heaven, all they can respond with is *"Holy!"* Then as they rotate around again, they catch a glimpse of something new and again cry, *"Holy! Holy! Holy! Holy!"* Each "holy" has an entirely different meaning. Each is a different response to something new they are seeing. Throughout eternity, God is continually revealing a new part of His nature that astounds us and motivates us to praise and worship.

He will continue building upon our revelation of who He really is. Perhaps every hour on the hour there will be a brand new explosion of praise within the people of God. It cannot get boring because we'll be looking and beholding the beauty of His face in reality, in that very moment. It will no longer be a spiritual thing "out there" that we have to move into through the gifts of the Holy Spirit. Instead we'll be sitting on His lap singing. I'm telling you, it can't get boring there!

Chapter Fourteen

The Symphony of Earth, The Symphony of Sound

If we are in constant agreement with the Word of God, we become instruments through which His sound is played. We become musical vessels and carriers of what in musical terms is called "sympathetic vibration." A good example of sympathetic vibration is when someone sets their guitar down on a stand. If you were to put your ear close to the guitar's body while other noises were being made in the room, you would hear a sound emanating from the instrument. For instance, if someone was talking, you would hear the guitar make a sound with each word spoken. This is because the vibration of the person's voice comes into "agreement" with the vibrations the guitar has the capability of producing.

The Greek word for this is *sumphoneo*, and means "to be harmonious, to agree or to be together with." It is where we get the word "symphony." In Matthew 18:19 Jesus says, *"Again I say to you that if two of you agree on earth concerning anything that they ask, it will be done for them by My Father in*

heaven." The word for agree there is *sumphoneo.*
In music that agreement is what makes up a chord.
A chord is simply tones of agreement. Two different
notes in agreement create harmony. If they are not in
agreement they create discord. That's why in
II Chronicles 5:13, it says they lifted up their voice *"to
make one sound."* They were in agreement, in
sumphoneo. Matthew 18:19 shows the validity of
agreement.

Agreement always touches heaven, for *"where
two or three are gathered together"* in Jesus' name,
He declares Himself *"in the midst of them"* (Matthew
18:20). That's why agreement with what God is saying
and doing, is so important. Agreement is a musical
principle. The definition for a chord is "a combination
of two or more sounds uttered at the same time,
according to the laws of harmony." In II Chronicles,
there were 4,000 musicians with instruments in
agreement, and you know what happened. In Acts 2,
there were 120 worshipers in agreement. You know
what happened. Heaven is full of worshipers in
agreement. If today we were able to bring together
a gathering that could truly come into agreement,
I wonder what would happen?

The Orchestra of God

Think of the kingdom of God as a massive band
or orchestra. Within that orchestra, there are
individual instruments or churches. Within each
individual instrument are many components. As an
example, let's look at a guitar. A quality guitar can be
constructed from materials gathered from around the

world. For instance, one of my guitars which I dearly love has the back and sides made of Brazilian rosewood. The fingerboard and bridge are made of ebony from the West Coast of Africa and from Sri Lanka. The neck is a Honduran mahogany, and its keys are made of silver from Germany. The pick-guard is tortoise shell from a tortoise somewhere (God only knows), and the top is sitka spruce from Alaska. The inlay on the neck is made of abalone from Australia, while the position dots are made out of pearl from an oyster shell found off the shores of Japan. The bridge plate is a wood called purple heart from South America. The rosette and herringbone purfling are made of German maple. The nut and saddle are made out of ivory from old fossilized mastodon tusks.

All of these components have been gathered, and each part has gone through its own unique process to finally come into shape as a completed guitar. Think about it. Somewhere in Brazil or Canada, a tree had to go through seasons of rain, of drought, of scorching heat or bone-chilling blizzards. After seeing generation after generation pass, the same tree eventually had to give its life for the sake of this instrument. Out of all the trees in the world, the tree was chosen based on the density of its grain, because a tree grown in the climate of Brazil is different than one grown in Alaska. Different weather conditions and climates develop different strengths and weaknesses in the fabric of the wood. In turn, this causes the various pieces of the guitar to respond differently to the frequencies and tones played.

Once the wood is harvested, it goes through a drying or dying process. Before the wood can be built into the guitar, it must be put into a controlled environment. For three years it is kept in one hundred degree heat and 30 percent relative humidity. This makes the wood more stable and enhances the tonal qualities once it's become an instrument of music. If it did not endure the heat of the drying process and was prematurely built into an instrument, the guitar would bend, warp, crack, and ultimately self-destruct when the tension of the strings was applied. Believe it or not, the tension applied to a neck and body of a guitar with medium gauge strings is about 165 pounds of pressure. It fluctuates as the guitar is played with more or less aggression. Either way, the guitar must be able to maintain stability no matter how, where, or when it's played. A guitar that cannot maintain stability will constantly be in and out of tune. It will bring an unpleasant sound to the listener and be an aggravation to the player. But when everything functions in agreement with each piece of wood rightly related one to another, *"fitly joined together," sumphoneo* is accomplished.

On a fine guitar, a master luthier understands the principles of tension, the characteristics of different woods and the tonal differences in mahogany versus rosewood, and rosewood versus walnut, etc. The brace inside a guitar is for the purpose of adding strength to the body. He understands that the brace can be off one inch and completely change the sound of the guitar and diminish the vibrations of the top. This diminishes its ability to produce tones of beauty and agreement. To bring all of the parts of a guitar into unity, every tree, every pearl, and every ounce of silver had to die, be brought out of its original state and restructured by molding, shaping, cutting, filing, melting, and sanding. It has to be altered from its original state and ultimately transformed into a new creation. The tree that died, and stood in a forest resisting the natural wind, has been recreated by the hand of the luthier, and resurrected to bring forth a new sound. The new sound is to be the expression of the heart of the musician agreeing with the sound of worship in heaven. It is sufficient to say, much has to be done to a tree for it to sing.

An Orchestra of Nations

Many times in Scripture, wood represents humanity. For instance, we are the *"trees of righteousness, the planting of the Lord"* (Isaiah 61:3). For a tree to become a guitar, much sawdust is created. There is much cutting away, filing, and sanding. The guitar's creation process parallels our individual lives. We have gone through the changes and various seasons of shaping and molding. It more appropriately pictures the local church. Throughout Scripture, God always moved as a result of unity and agreement. One definition of unity is corporate humility. Humility is nothing more than losing our identities for the purpose of unity and agreement with God. As we lose our identities in Him, we find a new identity as new creations in Christ Jesus. We may not all look alike—some may be ebony, some spruce, and some rosewood. We may come from the four corners of the earth.

This point remains: God will raise us up from different environments, circumstances, experiences, and from different parts of the world to interweave our lives with each other. The woman sitting next to you in church may be from Uganda, while the family sitting on the front row is from Hong Kong. Metropolitan areas such as Atlanta or New Orleans perfectly show this "melting pot" by bringing together every culture and subculture under one giant umbrella of a city. When we are continually reaching into our community with the gospel, the church in turn represents all the nations in that city.

But how did we all end up in the same place? How did the Ugandan woman or the family from Hong Kong end up at your church? Each person had to go through a certain transition, a certain adjustment to be part of the church. In the United States, the family from Hong Kong can't continue speaking Cantonese, but must adapt to the English language. Part of who they are must be shed in order to be part of the whole. Naturally, there are elements that cannot and should not be shed. The woman from Uganda cannot shed her darker skin, nor can the Chinese family shed their black hair. These are natural elements which God purposely made as unique parts of the kaleidoscope of the earth's cultures.

Think again of the components of a guitar. The back and sides of a guitar were not always simple slabs of wood. Years ago they were part of a majestic Brazilian rosewood that stood in a mighty forest. It took severe transformation to make that huge tree into the back of a guitar. The piece certainly doesn't have the regal look it had as a massive figure in the forest. Whereas, before it was without voice, now it can sing as a significant part of a fine instrument. As individuals we may no longer be trees, but instead a bridge plate. Or we may no longer be a beautiful raw pearl in an oyster shell, but are instead a position dot on the neck. As a church, we're made of the different components of an instrument. We have different colors, textures and innate abilities, yet we make up one unified instrument, or one church. Now, together—in *sumphoneo*—we can sing.

As we lose our identities, we're put in the posture of becoming a corporate church. Lest we become haughty and arrogant, we need to humble ourselves and realize there are other vital churches in our city. They are the other instruments in His orchestra. The church down the road doesn't look like a guitar or sound like a guitar, and isn't even made of the same fiber as a guitar. It is a flute, with a lilting whisper of the wind, creating beautiful tones of meditation. And the church down the road from that one is a trumpet that will blare forth a prophetic sound, declaring war upon the enemies. The church across the road is possibly a harp that brings the beautiful sounds of intimacy and worship. And the church across town is a tympani. This is one of the main reasons the Lord wants us to lose our identities on every level. Individually, on a local church level and on an extra-local level, we can't be arrogant and think we're special because we as a city have unified ourselves and put together a great meeting or conference. It would be worth our while to not be arrogant, but to truly humble ourselves as a city, so there might be a state-wide and national unity brought around the place of praise and worship. Then we will release the sound of heaven.

If we're looking at a city as an orchestra, we must also think of the sections involved. There could be ten trumpet churches in the city, ten guitar churches and eight tympani. After all, a corporate sound of praise is what God has been trying to build in us for years. If you remember in the days of the Old Testament prophets, there was not much attention given to individual salvation. It was a corporate salvation that encompassed all of God's people. I think God is reminding us of that now. We need each other to complete the sound, to bring all the tones, timbres, rhythms and melodic variations to the church. To take it further, Nashville does not sound like New York. New York does not sound like New Orleans. And New Orleans does not sound like Boston. The United States does not sound like Switzerland. Switzerland does not sound like Bangladesh, nor Bangladesh like Peru. The whole earth has the potential to sound like heaven.

The Song of the Nations

On the day David brought the ark of God, and placed it in the midst of the tent that would become known as the tabernacle of David, he appointed ministers of music to minister before the Ark of the Lord. The musicians were to record songs, and also to thank and praise the Lord God (see I Chronicles 16). On the first day of a 33-year, 24 hour-a-day worship service, David delivered the first psalm into the hand of Asaph, one of the chief musicians. Let me point out some of the highlights of the lyrics of this song. Starting in I Chronicles 16:8-12, 14-15). David sang:

Oh, give thanks to the Lord! Call upon His name; Make known His deeds among the peoples! Sing to Him, sing psalms to Him; Talk of all His wondrous works! Glory in His holy name; Let the hearts of those rejoice who seek the Lord! Seek the Lord and His strength; Seek his face evermore! Remember His marvelous works which He has done, His wonders and the judgments of His mouth, He is the Lord our God; His judgments are in ALL the earth. Remember His covenant always, the word which He commanded for a thousand generations.

It sounds like a pretty serious song, doesn't it? Look at verse 23-25: "Sing to the Lord, ALL the earth; Proclaim the good news of His salvation from day to day. Declare His glory among the nations, His wonders among all peoples. For the Lord is great and greatly to be praised." And in verse 31, "Let the heavens rejoice, and let the earth be glad; And let them say among the nations, 'The Lord reigns.'" Notice how much the nations were emphasized in the lyrics of this song. And remember, it *was* a song. David said in Psalm 57:7 *"My heart is steadfast, O God, my heart is steadfast; I will sing and give praise. Awake, my glory! Awake lute and harp! I will awaken the dawn, I will praise You, O Lord, among the peoples; I will sing to You among the nations. For Your mercy reaches unto the heavens, And Your truth unto the clouds. Be exalted, O God, above the heavens; Let Your glory be above all the earth."* As stated earlier, David said he would *sing* what he saw.

May we begin to sing what we see. Truly we are in a day of a new revelation that is not new at all. It is only a *fresh* release of the prophetic coming to the sounds that are seen and heard in God's people. So may the harps, psalteries, guitars, trumpets, banjos, ukuleles, and tubas that have been fashioned as instruments of praise begin to declare the glory above all the earth.

David sang lyrics and declared that release of the Lord over his nation and the nations of the world. Haven't we been given the same lyric? Do we not have the same God of the nations dwelling in our fixed hearts that David had? Are we not the last days generation in which God has declared He will rebuild the tabernacle of David? Therefore, we have the responsibility and ability to respond in agreement to the call and the anointing on us as a people. We are the generation that must show forth the praises of God, and release His glory in the earth.

I believe that we are instruments fashioned for the purpose of high praises unto our God. If you go to an opera or ballet, the stage is set for the visual show. The orchestra finds itself in a pit, only creating a supporting background for the visual performance of the dancers. But I believe that the real orchestra of the spirit is no longer in the pit, it's on stage.

Preparing the Orchestra

If you've ever had the opportunity to hear a major symphony, you know the power and impact it can have upon the emotions of an audience. With the rise and fall of dynamics, beauty comes from the masterpieces composed over the centuries. When I go to a symphony, it is intriguing what takes place before they start: the hustle and bustle, the rustling of papers, the scurrying of musicians, the squeaks and squawks of the woodwinds tuning, the moaning of the double basses and the last minute preparations of the percussion section. After twenty to thirty minutes of the sounds of pandemonium, the conductor gives three simple taps of the baton upon the podium. Immediately everything comes to attention. A massive sound of unity and agreement is suddenly heard, whereas ten seconds earlier, the sound of dissonance and disagreement dominated the room. Three little clicks on the podium changed everything. As the conductor's hands are raised, the downbeat is imminent. Hustle and bustle gives way to order, as every eye in the orchestra focuses on the conductor. With his gestures and facial expressions, he conducts the dynamics of each section of the orchestra. With his hand, he mixes and blends the music as it is being played. To start, however, we hear a simple first tap of the conductor's baton. *Click.*

The physical setup of an orchestra gives every player a clear line of vision to the conductor. From the flutist to the cellist, every member of the orchestra must have the ability to simultaneously see their music and the conductor. A music stand is positioned so that a musician hardly has to move his eyes from the score, and can simply stare over the top of his pages to see the next instruction from the conductor. God has given us His Word as our music. As a church, we have rehearsed it over and over again. But in order to play in agreement with God's instructions—in *sumphoneo* with His direction—we must keep our eyes on the conductor of all men, Jesus Christ. We must keep a clear line of vision to see His command of when we should come in, when we should back off a little, or when we should play a phrase with every ounce of energy in us. To sound the music of His Word, we must be in complete accordance with His conducting. I venture to say that if we listen closely, we can hear the second click of a heavenly baton calling every eye to Him. *Click. Click.* May we be in tune.

The difference between a warrior and a wimp is simple. When the heat of battle comes, the wimp folds and the warrior focuses. As individuals warm up in a corporate sound of dissonance, the conductor gives opportunity for the preparation, the hustle and bustle, the shaping, molding, and fine tuning of each instrument. We've come to the place now that two clicks have been heard. Before the third click is sounded, we must determine in our hearts whether we are wimps or warriors. On the third click, we must be ready to release the thunder of a pure tone. Immediately after the third click is heard, His hands are raised to signify an inhaling. When the conductor's hands come down, it will be the prompting to exhale a blast of the wind of the Spirit and jolt the enemies of God into submission to His authority in us.

Before the Conductor's arms swing down in a sweeping motion to start the music, every player must know his place. No more wishy-washy personality conflicts of wondering if you're in the right section, or even in the right orchestra. Every musician has a purpose and a holy assurance of his important and needed role to the entire orchestra. As the members of David's orchestra spent their entire lives creating, molding, and shaping their instruments to become extensions of themselves, our lives must be the instruments of our worship. Through this, our place in His orchestra is sure.

Have you ever wondered what use an orchestra would possibly have for a piccolo? The piccolo has consistently been an instrument of revolution. It has been the aggressive cry, the front-leader of warriors marching in a unified purpose to declare war against their enemy. In the spirit, the piccolo is a foghorn. Behind the sounds of the piccolo and drum of the revolutionary war beat the heart of a people willing to give their lives for their beliefs. The very truth that we yawn about today, they gave their blood for yesterday. The living faith of the dead has become the dead faith of the living. But God wants to release a sound within us that will bring resurrection to the church. We have to begin to see ourselves as a corporate sound, a *people* who have humbled ourselves and sought the face of God.

Though some of us are mined as silver out of Germany, we have to lose our identities as Germans. Though some were once mighty rosewood trees in a Brazilian forest, now we find ourselves as a plain slab of wood on the back of a guitar. Though we maintain some individual qualities, we have to humble ourselves to come into unity and agreement with some of the other components that make up the church, or the guitar, if you will. With this in mind, let me paraphrase a song we all know. It's the 133rd song in the book of Psalms: *"Now see how good and how pleasant it is to have lost our identities as a result of the molding, shaping, chiseling, and sanding of the hand of God on our lives that would cause us to become one instrument, united for the purpose of coming into agreement with the sound of heaven—the sound of corporate worship that requires corporate humility. And as God plays through His Body, both corporately and individually, may the sound of heaven and the symphony of earth resound its never-ending praise to Him."*

The Father is eager to release into our earthly realm sounds of heaven that will radically change the corporate walk of the church. These supernatural sounds contain the powerful essence of His creative voice and nature. As God's people come together with one unified voice to worship Him, the sounds of our praises will rise to His throne as a powerful symphony from the earth. I believe His response to earth's symphony will be an outpouring of the sounds of heaven both in us and the creation around us. The eternal praises, the sound of heaven, will merge with the symphony of earth. Let's individually and corporately pursue the high praises of God, giving ourselves to the worship of Jesus. As we do, we will enter the realm of the sounds of heaven, and the sounds of heaven will enter the realm of the earth. Our God will then receive the praise and honor of which He is so worthy.

For additional helpful sources of reading on topics covered in this book, please read:

Bauer, Marion, and Ethel Peyser, *How Music Grew,* Putnam, New York, 1939.

Burk, Cassie, et al., *America's Musical Heritage,* Laidlaw, New York, 1942.

Forbes, George, *William Wallace: Freedom Fighter,* Lang Syne, Glasgow, 1996.

Geiringer, Karl, *Musical Instruments,* Trans. Bernard Miall, Oxford UP, New York, 1945.

Grame, Theodore, *America's Ethnic Music,* Cultural Maintenance, Tarpon Springs, 1976.

Howard, John Tasker, and George Kent Bellows, *A Short History of Music in America,* New York, 1957.

Leichtentritt, Hugo, *Music, History and Ideas,* Harvard UP, Cambridge, 1946.

Lomax, Alan, *The Folk Songs of North America,* Doubleday, New York, 1960.

Machlis, Joseph, *The Enjoyment of Music,* Norton & Co., New York, 1955.

Oliver, Paul, *The Story of Blues,* Chilton, New York, 1969.

Paterson, John, *The Praises of Israel,* Scribner, New York, 1950.

Scott, Sir Walter, *Scotland,* Collier, New York, 1829.

Small, Stephen, *An Irish Century: 1845-1945,* Barnes & Noble, New York, 1998.

Tyack, Rev. G.S., *A Book About Bells,* Andrews & Co., London, 1898.

Wood, Alex, *The Physical Basis of Music,* Cambridge UP, Cambridge, 1913.